365 Easy Fast Recipes

Great Tasting
Recipes in 30 Minutes or Less

365 Easy, Fast Recipes

1st Printing January 2007

Copyright © 2007
By Cookbook Resources LLC, Highland Village, Texas.
All rights reserved

ISBN 978-1-931294-80-5

Manufactured in China
Edited, Designed and Published in the
United States of America by
Cookbook Resources, LLC
541 Doubletree Drive
Highland Village, Texas 75077
Toll free 866-229-2665
www.cookbookresources.com

cookbook
resources® LLC
Bringing Families To The Table

Introduction

GONE ARE THE DAYS of working 9 to 5 and arriving home in time to watch the evening news. Now we rush to work in the wee hours of the morning, arrive home in time to cart the kids to gymnastics or soccer and grocery shop once a week—if we're lucky. Minutes with the family have become precious commodities we don't have to spare.

This is precisely why we are bringing you *365 Easy, Fast Recipes*. Inside you will find page after page of quick, simple solutions, reducing time spent in the kitchen and increasing the quality time gathered with family and friends. Study after study shows that children who regularly eat meals with their family excel in school and have fewer behavior problems.

Is the nest finally empty? Just because you have extra time, doesn't mean you have to spend it in the kitchen. Use the time saved taking advantage of these recipes to take care of all those honey-dos you swore you would accomplish once junior went off to college.

Whether you are searching for what to prepare for Monday night's supper; Friday evening's guests; Saturday afternoon's party; or Sunday morning breakfast with the family, *365 Easy, Fast Recipes* has the meal idea for you.

Contents

Munchies 25

Breads 55

Soups 73

Sandwiches 93

Side Dishes 107

Vegetables 117

Desserts 187

Cakes 197

Pies and Cobblers 203

Cookies 211

Candies 223

Easy Fast
Appetizers

Hearty Man's Favorite Dip

1 pound lean ground beef
½ pound hot pork sausage
1 (8 ounce) jar hot salsa
1 (32 ounce) carton cubed processed cheese

- Brown ground beef and sausage in large skillet. Stir until meats crumble and drain.
- Add salsa and cheese. Cook over low heat and stir constantly until cheese melts.
- Serve warm with chips.

Bean Dip Deluxe

2 (15 ounce) cans bean dip
1 pound lean ground beef, cooked
1 (4 ounce) can green chiles
1 cup hot salsa
1½ cups shredded cheddar cheese

- Layer bean dip, ground beef, chiles and salsa in 3-quart baking dish and top with cheese.
- Bake at 350° just until cheese melts, about 10 or 15 minutes.
- Serve with tortilla chips.

Ladies' Veggie Dip

You will hear the family saying, "You mean this is spinach?"

1 (10 ounce) package frozen chopped spinach, thawed, well
    drained
1 bunch fresh green onions with tops, chopped
1 (1 ounce) packet dry vegetable soup mix
1 tablespoon lemon juice
2 (8 ounce) cartons sour cream

- Squeeze spinach in paper towels to drain thoroughly.
- In medium bowl, combine all ingredients and add a little
  salt. (Adding several drops of hot sauce is also good.)
- Cover and refrigerate.
- Serve with chips.

Midwest Guacamole Dip

3 large ripe avocados, mashed
1 tablespoon fresh lemon juice
1 (1 ounce) package dry onion soup mix
1 (8 ounce) carton sour cream

- Combine avocados with lemon juice.
- Stir in soup mix and sour cream. (Add a little salt if
  desired.)
- Serve with chips or crackers.

Creamy Crunchy Spinach Dip

1 (10 ounce) package frozen chopped spinach, thawed
2 (8 ounce) packages cream cheese, softened
1 (1 ounce) package dry vegetable soup mix
1 (8 ounce) can water chestnuts, chopped

- Squeeze spinach in several paper towels to drain thoroughly.
- In mixing bowl, beat cream cheese until smooth. Fold in spinach, soup mix and water chestnuts and chill.
- Serve with chips or crackers.

Nutty Green Grass Dip

1 (14 ounce) can asparagus spears, drained, chopped
½ cup mayonnaise
¼ teaspoon hot sauce
½ cup chopped pecans

- Combine all ingredients in medium bowl and chill.
- Serve with wheat crackers.

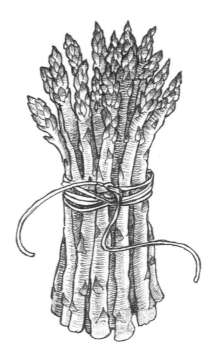

Bacon Dip

1 (14 ounce) jar marinated artichoke hearts, drained,
   chopped
1 cup mayonnaise
2 teaspoons Worcestershire sauce
5 slices bacon, cooked crisp, crumbled

- In large bowl, combine all ingredients.
- Pour into buttered 8-inch baking dish.
- Bake at 350° for 12 minutes.
- Serve hot with crackers.

Easy Clam Dip

1 (8 ounce) and 1 (3 ounce) package cream cheese
1/4 cup (1/2 stick) butter
2 (6 ounce) cans minced clams, drained
1/2 teaspoon Worcestershire sauce

- Melt cream cheese and butter in double boiler.
- Add minced clams and Worcestershire sauce.
- Serve hot.

Horsey Shrimp Dip

1 (6 ounce) can tiny, cooked shrimp, chopped, drained

3 tablespoons cream-style horseradish

⅓ cup mayonnaise

½ teaspoon Cajun seasoning

- Combine shrimp, horseradish, mayonnaise and seasoning.
- Chill and serve with crackers.

Shrimp Stuff

1 (8 ounce) package cream cheese, softened

½ cup mayonnaise

1 (6 ounce) can tiny, cooked shrimp, drained

1¼ teaspoons Creole (or Cajun) seasoning

1 tablespoon lemon juice

- Blend cream cheese and mayonnaise in mixing bowl until creamy.
- Add shrimp, seasoning and lemon juice and whip only until they mix well.
- Serve with chips.

Best Crab Dip Ever

1 (16 ounce) package cubed processed cheese
2 (6 ounce) cans crabmeat, drained, flaked
1 bunch fresh green onions with tops, chopped
2 cups mayonnaise
$\frac{1}{2}$ teaspoon seasoned salt

- Melt cheese in top of double boiler. Add crabmeat, onions, mayonnaise and seasoned salt.
- Serve hot or at room temperature with assorted crackers.

Don't count on your guests leaving the table until this dip is gone!

So Easy Crab Dip

1 (6 ounce) can white crabmeat, drained, flaked
1 (8 ounce) package cream cheese
$\frac{1}{2}$ cup (1 stick) butter

- In saucepan, combine crabmeat, cream cheese and butter.
- Heat and mix thoroughly.
- Transfer to hot chafing dish. Serve with chips.

Apple Cream Cheese Dip

1 (8 ounce) package cream cheese, softened
2 tablespoons powdered sugar
3 tablespoons orange juice concentrate, thawed
1 teaspoon ground cinnamon

- In mixing bowl, combine all ingredients and mix until well blended.

Extra Special Guacamole

4 medium avocados, peeled
3 tablespoons sour cream
1 tablespoon hot sauce
1½ teaspoons garlic salt
2 teaspoons lemon juice
2 tablespoons Italian salad dressing

- In bowl, mash avocados to desired smoothness and stir in sour cream, hot sauce, garlic salt, lemon juice and Italian dressing. You may want to taste to determine if you need extra salt. Serve with chips.

Creamy Bean Dip

1 (3 ounce) package cream cheese, softened

2 (15 ounce) cans cannellini (or navy) beans, drained

1 heaping teaspoon prepared minced garlic

¼ cup extra-virgin olive oil

2 teaspoons fresh, minced rosemary

Grated zest of 1 lemon

- Place cream cheese, beans, garlic and salt to taste, in bowl of food processor. Turn machine on and add olive oil in a steady stream and process until smooth.

- Place mixture in bowl and stir in minced rosemary and lemon zest. You might taste and add more salt if necessary. Refrigerate.

Leftover Ham Dip

¾ cup smooth peanut butter

2 tablespoons soy sauce

½ cup honey

3 tablespoons lime juice

- In bowl, combine all dip ingredients, mixing well.

- Cut ham in bite-size chunks and use toothpicks for ham and dip-dip-dip!

Steamy Artichoke Dip

1 (14 ounce) can artichoke, drained, chopped

1¼ cups mayonnaise (not light)

1 cup grated parmesan cheese

2 teaspoons minced garlic

- Preheat oven to 350°. In bowl, combine artichokes, mayonnaise, parmesan and garlic, mixing well.

- Spoon into an 8 or 9-inch Pyrex® pie pan and bake uncovered for 25 minutes. Serve hot with wheat crackers.

Cheesy Onion Dip

1 (3 ounce) package cream cheese, softened, cut into chunks

⅔ cup mayonnaise

1 sweet yellow onion (Vidalia if available), finely chopped

1 (12 ounce) package shredded cheddar cheese

½ teaspoon dried thyme

- Preheat oven to 350°. Beat together cream cheese and mayonnaise, until mixture blends well. Stir in onions.

- In bowl, combine onion-cream cheese mixture, cheddar cheese and dried thyme. Spoon into a shallow baking dish; cover and bake 20 minutes. Cool slightly and serve with round buttery crackers.

Sweet 'n Cheesy-Garlic Spread

2 (8 ounce) packages cream cheese, softened
1/4 cup apricot preserves
1 teaspoon minced garlic
1/4 cup finely chopped walnuts
3 fresh green onions, finely chopped (only green portion)

- In mixing bowl, combine cream cheese and apricot preserves and beat until well blended. Stir in garlic, walnuts and green onions. Refrigerate until ready to use.
- Serve with assorted crackers.

Easy Olive Spread

1 (8 ounce) package cream cheese, softened
1/3 cup mayonnaise
3/4 cup chopped pecans
1 cup chopped green olives, drained
1/4 teaspoon black pepper

- In mixing bowl, blend cream cheese and mayonnaise until smooth.
- Add pecans, olives and black pepper, mix well and refrigerate.
- Serve on crackers or make sandwiches with party rye bread.

Doctored Bean Dip

1 (15 ounce) can Mexican-style chili beans
½ teaspoon ground cumin
½ teaspoon chili powder
¼ teaspoon dried oregano

- Drain beans and reserve 2 tablespoons liquid.
- Combine beans, reserved liquid, cumin, chili powder and oregano in food processor. Pulse several times until beans are partially chopped.
- Pour mixture into small saucepan and cook over low heat, stirring constantly until thoroughly heated.

Quesadillas in a Flash

¼ cup ricotta cheese, divided
6 (6 inch) corn tortillas
⅔ cup shredded Monterey Jack cheese, divided
1 (4 ounce) can diced green chiles, drained

- Spread 1 tablespoon ricotta over tortilla. Add 1 heaping tablespoon cheese and 1 tablespoon chiles. Place second tortilla on top.
- Repeat to make 2 more quesadillas.
- In heated skillet, add 1 quesadilla and cook for 3 minutes on each side.
- Remove from heat and cut into 4 wedges. Repeat with remaining quesadillas.
- Serve warm with salsa.

Speedy Gonzales Queso

1 (16 ounce) package cubed processed cheese
½ cup milk
1 (12 ounce) jar salsa, divided

- In saucepan, melt cheese and milk in double boiler.
- Add about half of salsa.
- Serve with tortilla chips.

Orange Party Spread

2 (8 ounce) packages cream cheese, softened
½ cup powdered sugar
1 tablespoon grated orange peel
2 tablespoons Grand Marnier
2 tablespoons frozen orange juice concentrate

- Blend all ingredients in mixing bowl until smooth and refrigerate.
- Spread on dessert breads to make sandwiches.

This spread is great on poppy seed buns and may also be used as dip for fruit.

Tangy Artichoke Dip

½ cup (1 stick) butter
1 (14 ounce) can artichoke hearts, drained, chopped
1 (4 ounce) package blue cheese
2 teaspoons lemon juice

- In skillet, melt butter and mix in artichoke hearts.
- Add blue cheese and lemon juice.
- Serve hot in chaffing dish.

English Muffin Bites

2 (8 ounce) packages cream cheese, softened
¼ cup mayonnaise
2 tablespoons white wine Worcestershire sauce
2 cups finely shredded, cooked chicken breasts
¼ cup chopped almonds, toasted
English Muffins

- In mixing bowl, combine cream cheese, mayonnaise and Worcestershire sauce and beat until creamy.
- Fold in shredded chicken and almonds.
- Spread on English muffin halves and toast. (Do not brown.)

Snappy Shrimp Bites

1 (6 ounce) can shrimp, drained, chopped
1 cup mayonnaise
1 cup shredded cheddar cheese
10 to 12 slices white bread, trimmed, cut in squares

• Combine shrimp, mayonnaise and cheese and mix well.
• Spread shrimp mixture on bread squares and broil until bubbly.

Pepperoni Rounds

1 (5 ounce) box melba rounds
¾ cup chili sauce
5 ounces pepperoni rounds
1 cup shredded mozzarella cheese

• Spread melba rounds with chili sauce.
• Top melba rounds with pepperoni slices and sprinkle with cheese.
• Bake on baking sheet at 375° for 3 to 5 minutes.

Sweet Little Smokies

1 cup ketchup
1 cup plum jelly
1 tablespoon lemon juice
4 tablespoons prepared mustard
2 (5 ounce) packages tiny smoked sausages

- In saucepan, combine ketchup, jelly, lemon juice and mustard, heat and mix well.
- Add sausages and simmer for 10 minutes. Serve hot with cocktail toothpicks.

Southwest Turkey Pizza

4 (8-inch) flour tortillas

Topping:

2 cups deli smoked turkey, diced
1 (11 ounce) can mexicorn, drained
1 (15 ounce) can black beans, rinsed, drainedg
2 tablespoons lemon juice
1 cup Monterey Jack cheese with jalapeno peppersl

- Preheat oven to 350°. Place tortillas on greased baking sheet and bake 10 minutes or until edges are light brown. Remove from oven, stack and press down to flatten.
- In skillet with a little oil, combine diced turkey, corn and black beans. Heat, stirring constantly until mixture is thoroughly hot; stir in lime juice.
- Place tortillas on baking sheet and spoon about ¾ cup turkey-corn mixture on each tortilla. Sprinkle cheese on top of each pizza and return to oven for 2 minutes or just until cheese melts.

Cheesy Drops

2 cups biscuit mix

⅓ cup sour cream

1 egg

1 (4 ounce) can chopped green chilies, drained

1½ cups shredded sharp cheddar cheese

- Preheat oven to 375°. In bowl, combine biscuit mix, sour cream, egg and green chilies and mix until well blended. Stir in cheese, mixture will be thick.

- Drop by heaping teaspoons onto a greased baking sheet. Bake 10 minutes or until golden brown. Serve warm.

Border Barter

1 (16 ounce) package shredded cheddar cheese

1 (5 ounce) can evaporated milk

1 teaspoon cumin

1 tablespoon chili powder

1 (10 ounce) can tomatoes and green chiles

- Melt cheese with evaporated milk in double boiler.

- In blender, mix cumin, chili powder and tomatoes and green chiles. (Add dash of garlic powder if you like.)

- Add tomato mixture to melted cheese and mix well.

- Serve hot with chips.

Chile Queso

1 (15 ounce) can chili without beans
1 (10 ounce) can tomatoes and green chiles
1 (16 ounce) package cubed processed cheese
1/2 cup chopped green onions
1/2 teaspoon cayenne pepper

- In saucepan, combine all ingredients.
- Heat just until cheese melts and stir constantly.
- Serve warm with assorted dippers or toasted French bread sticks.

Meatballs on a Stick

1 (14 ounce) package frozen cooked meatballs, thawed
1 tablespoon soy sauce
1/2 cup chili sauce
2/3 cup grape or plum jelly
1/4 cup dijon-style mustard

- In skillet, cook meatballs in soy sauce until heated through.
- Combine chili sauce, jelly and mustard and pour over meatballs.
- Cook and stir until jelly dissolves and mixture comes to a boil.
- Reduce heat, cover and simmer for about 5 minutes.

Be sure to have toothpicks ready for serving.

Hot Reubens Squares

½ cup thousand island dressing

24 slices party rye bread

1⅓ cups well drained, chopped sauerkraut

½ pound thinly sliced corned beef

¼ pound sliced Swiss cheese

- Spread dressing on slices of bread.
- Place 1 slice corned beef on bread and top with sauerkraut.
- Cut cheese same size as bread and place over sauerkraut.
- Place open-face sandwiches on baking sheet and bake at 375° for 10 minutes or until cheese melts.

Easy Beef and Chips

1 (8 ounce) package cream cheese, softened

1 (8 ounce) carton sour cream

1 (3 ounce) package dried beef, cubed

½ cup finely chopped pecans

- Use mixer to beat cream cheese and sour cream until smooth and creamy.
- Fold in dried beef chunks and pecans.
- Chill and serve with chips.

Guacamole Mash

4 avocados, peeled
½ cup salsa
¼ cup sour cream
1 teaspoon salt

- Split avocados and remove seeds. Mash avocado with fork.
- Add salsa, sour cream and salt and stir.
- Serve with tortilla chips.

Garlic-Beef Ball

1 (8 ounce) package cream cheese, softened
2 teaspoons horseradish
1 teaspoon prepared mustard
¼ teaspoon garlic powder
1 (5 ounce) package dried beef, finely chopped

- In mixing bowl, blend cream cheese, horseradish, mustard and garlic powder and roll into ball.
- Roll ball in dried beef. (The best way to chop dried beef is with scissors.)
- Serve with crackers.

Flash-in-the-Pan Sausage Balls

1 pound hot pork sausage, uncooked
1 (16 ounce) package grated cheddar cheese
3 cups biscuit mix
⅓ cup milk

- Combine all ingredients and form into small balls. (If dough is a little too sticky, add 1 more teaspoon biscuit mix.)
- Bake at 375° for 13 to 15 minutes.

Olive Drops

2¼ cups shredded sharp cheddar cheese
1 cup flour
½ cup (1 stick) butter, melted
1 (5 ounce) jar green olives

- In large bowl, combine cheese and flour. Add butter and mix well.
- Cover olives with mixture and form into balls.
- Bake at 350° for about 15 minutes or until light brown.

Easy Cheese Ball Bites

½ cup (1 stick) butter, softened
1 (6 ounce) jar sharp processed cheese spread, softened
¼ teaspoon cayenne pepper
½ teaspoon salt
1 cup plus 2 tablespoons flour

- In bowl, mix butter, cheese spread, cayenne pepper and salt and work flour in gradually.
- Form into marble-size balls and flatten with fork.
- Bake at 400° for 6 to 8 minutes or until light brown.

Orange-Fruit Dip

1 (8 ounce) package cream cheese, softened
1 (8 ounce) carton orange yogurt
½ cup orange marmalade
¼ cup finely chopped pecans

- Use mixer to beat cream cheese until smooth.
- Fold in yogurt, marmalade and pecans and chill.
- Serve with apple slices.

Brown Sugar Betty

1 (8 ounce) package cream cheese, softened

1 cup packed brown sugar

1 teaspoon vanilla extract

1 cup finely chopped pecans

- In small mixing bowl combine cream cheese, sugar and vanilla and beat until smooth.
- Stir in pecans.
- Serve with sliced apples for dipping.

Juicy Fruit

Delicious!

1 (8 ounce) package cream cheese, softened

2 (7 ounce) jars marshmallow cream

$\frac{1}{2}$ teaspoon cinnamon

$\frac{1}{8}$ teaspoon ground ginger

- With mixer, combine and beat all ingredients.
- Mix well and refrigerate.
- Serve with unpeeled slices of nectarines or apple slices.

Easy Fast
Munchies

Nutty Mix

1 pound mixed nuts
¼ cup maple syrup
2 tablespoons brown sugar
1 (1 ounce) package dry ranch-style salad dressing mix

- In bowl, combine nuts and maple syrup and mix well.
- Sprinkle with brown sugar and salad dressing mix and stir gently to coat.
- Spread in greased 10 x 15-inch baking pan.
- Bake at 300° for 25 minutes or until light brown and cool.

Daddy-O Pecans

¼ cup (½ stick) butter, melted
1 tablespoon Worcestershire sauce
2 cups pecan halves
¼ teaspoon cayenne pepper

- In mixing bowl, combine butter and Worcestershire sauce and mix well.
- Add pecans, cayenne pepper and ¼ teaspoon salt.
- Stir and toss pecans until well coated.
- Roast on baking sheet at 350° for 15 minutes. Stir or shake pan occasionally.

Double-Sugar Pecans

$\frac{1}{2}$ cup packed brown sugar

$\frac{1}{4}$ cup sugar

$\frac{1}{2}$ cup sour cream

$\frac{1}{8}$ teaspoon salt

3 cups pecan halves

- Combine sugars and sour cream and stir over medium heat until sugar dissolves.
- Boil sugar-sour cream mixture to soft-ball stage, add salt and remove from heat.
- Add pecans, stir to coat and pour on wax paper.
- Separate pecans carefully. (They will harden after several minutes.)

Butterscotch Munchies

1 (12 ounce) package butterscotch morsels

2 cups chow mein noodles

1 cup dry-roasted peanuts

- In saucepan, heat butterscotch morsels over low heat until they completely melt.
- Add noodles and peanuts and stir until each piece is coated.
- Drop by teaspoonfuls on wax paper.
- Cool and store in airtight container.

• •

Cinnamon Pecans

1 pound shelled pecan halves

1 egg white, slightly beaten with fork

2 tablespoons cinnamon

¾ cup sugar

- Combine pecan halves with egg white and mix well.
- Sprinkle with mixture of cinnamon and sugar and stir until all pecans are coated.
- Spread on baking sheet and bake at 325° for about 20 minutes.
- Cool and store in covered container.

Favorite Nut Snacks

You can't eat just one!

2 cups sugar

2 teaspoons cinnamon

1 teaspoon ground nutmeg

½ teaspoon ground cloves

4 cups pecan halves

- Combine sugar, cinnamon, nutmeg, cloves, ½ cup water and ¼ teaspoon salt.
- Mix well, cover with wax paper and microwave on HIGH for 4 minutes.
- Stir and microwave another 4 minutes.
- Add pecans, quickly mix well and spread on wax paper to cool.
- Break apart and store in covered container.

Potato Stick Crunch

1 (12 ounce) can salted peanuts
1 (7 ounce) can potato sticks, broken up
3 cups butterscotch chips
3 tablespoons peanut butter

- Combine peanuts and potato sticks in bowl and set aside.
- In microwave, heat butterscotch chips and peanut butter at 70% power for 1 to 2 minutes or until they melt and stir every 30 seconds.
- Add butterscotch mixture to peanut mixture and stir to coat evenly.
- Drop by rounded tablespoonfuls on wax paper-lined baking sheet.
- Refrigerate until set, about 10 minutes.

Sweet Salties

8 (2 ounce) squares almond bark
1 (12 ounce) package salted Spanish peanuts
3 cups thin pretzel sticks, broken up

- Place almond bark in top of double boiler, heat and stir until almond bark melts.
- Remove from heat and cool 2 minutes.
- Add peanuts and pretzels and stir until coated.
- Drop by teaspoonfuls on wax paper and chill 20 minutes or until firm.

Easy Fast
Beverages

Fruity Party Punch

1 (46 ounce) can pineapple juice

2 (46 ounce) cans apple juice

3 quarts ginger ale

Fresh mint to garnish, optional

- Combine pineapple juice and apple juice and make ice ring with part of juice.
- Chill remaining juice mixture and ginger ale.
- When ready to serve, combine juice mixture and ginger ale and place ice ring in punch bowl.

If you don't have a round gelatin mold with hole in the middle, make the ice ring with any type of gelatin mold.

Red Fizzy

1 (46 ounce) can pineapple-grapefruit juice

$\frac{1}{2}$ cup sugar

$\frac{1}{4}$ cup cinnamon candies

1 quart ginger ale, chilled

- In large saucepan, combine pineapple-grapefruit juice, sugar and candies. Bring to a boil and stir until candies dissolve.
- Cool until time to serve and stir occasionally to completely dissolve candies.
- Add ginger ale just before serving.

Tropical Delight

1 (46 ounce) can pineapple juice, chilled
1 (20 ounce) can crushed pineapple with juice
1 (15 ounce) can cream of coconut
1 (32 ounce) bottle lemon-lime carbonated drink, chilled

- Combine all ingredients.
- Serve over ice cubes.

Party-Time Splash

1 (46 ounce) can pineapple juice
1 (46 ounce) can apple juice
3 quarts ginger ale, chilled

- Freeze pineapple and apple juices in their cans.
- One hour before serving, set out cans at room temperature.
- When ready to serve, place pineapple and apple juices in punch bowl and add chilled ginger ale. Stir to mix.

Sunny Fruit Mix

1 (46 ounce) can pineapple juice, chilled
1 quart apple juice, chilled
1 (2 liter) bottle lemon-lime carbonated beverage, chilled
1 (6 ounce) can frozen lemonade concentrate, thawed
1 orange, sliced

- Combine pineapple juice, apple juice, lemon-lime beverage and lemonade in punch bowl.
- Add orange slices for decoration.

Florida Sunshine

3 cups sugar
6 cups orange juice, chilled
6 cups grapefruit juice, chilled
1½ cups lime juice, chilled
1 liter ginger ale, chilled

- In saucepan, bring sugar and 2 cups water to boil and cook for 5 minutes. Cover and refrigerate until cool.
- Combine juices and sugar mixture and mix well.
- Just before serving, stir in ginger ale. Serve over ice.

Lime Ale

1 (46 ounce) can pineapple juice

1 (46 ounce) can apricot nectar

3 (6 ounce) cans frozen limeade concentrate, thawed

3 quarts ginger ale, chilled

- Combine pineapple juice, apricot nectar and limeade concentrate and chill.
- When ready to serve, add ginger ale.

Celebration Punch

1 (750 ml) bottle dry white wine, chilled

1 cup apricot brandy

1 cup triple sec

2 (750 ml) bottles dry champagne, chilled

2 quarts club soda

- In large pitcher, combine white wine, apricot brandy and triple sec. Cover and chill until ready to use.
- At serving time, add champagne and club soda, stir to blend and pour in punch bowl.
- Add ice ring to punch bowl and serve.

Strawberry Smoothie

2 bananas, peeled, sliced
1 pint fresh strawberries, washed, quartered
1 (8 ounce) container strawberry yogurt
¼ cup orange juice

- Place all ingredients in blender. Process until smooth.

Strawberry-Banana Shake

1 (10 ounce) package frozen strawberries, partially thawed
2 bananas, sliced in 1-inch pieces
1 cup half-and-half cream
½ cup sugar
1 quart vanilla ice cream

- In blender, combine strawberries, bananas, cream and sugar. Cover and blend at high speed for about 30 seconds.
- Add ice cream and blend for about 45 seconds. Serve immediately.

Orange Slushie

1 (20 ounce) can crushed pineapple with juice

½ cup frozen pina colada concentrate

1 pint orange sherbet

½ cup orange juice

- Combine all ingredients in blender. Cover and blend on high speed until smooth.
- Serve immediately in sherbet glasses.

Watermelon Smoothie

About 2 cups watermelon cubes, seeded

2 tablespoons honey

Dash of cinnamon

1 (8 ounce) carton lemon yogurt

- With blender, puree watermelon, honey and cinnamon quickly, being careful not to over blend. Pulse in lemon yogurt and serve immediately.

Strawberry Patch Breeze

1 (10 ounce) package frozen strawberries, thawed
½ gallon strawberry ice cream, softened
2 (2 liter) bottles ginger ale, chilled
Fresh strawberries, optional

- Process frozen strawberries in blender.
- Combine strawberries, chunks of ice cream and ginger ale in punch bowl.
- Stir and serve immediately.
- Garnish with fresh strawberries.

Coffee Milk Shake Punch

This is so good you will want a big glass of it instead of a punch cup full.

1 gallon very strong, brewed coffee
½ cup sugar
3 tablespoons vanilla extract
2 pints half-and-half cream
1 gallon vanilla ice cream, softened

- Add sugar to coffee and chill. (Add more sugar if you like it sweeter.)
- Add vanilla and half-and-half.
- When ready to serve, combine coffee mixture and ice cream in punch bowl. Break up ice cream into chunks.

Orange-Cream Slush

2 cups orange juice

$\frac{1}{2}$ cup instant, non-fat dry milk

$\frac{1}{4}$ teaspoon almond extract

8 ice cubes

- Combine all ingredients in blender and process on high until mixture is smooth and thick.
- Serve immediately.

Festive Party Nog

1 gallon egg nog

1 pint whipping cream

1 quart brandy

$\frac{1}{2}$ gallon vanilla ice cream, softened

- Combine all ingredients and mix well.
- Serve in individual cups, sprinkle with nutmeg and serve immediately.

Summertime Fizz

1 $\frac{1}{4}$ cups amaretto

2 quarts cold orange juice

1 (15 ounce) bottle club soda, chilled

Orange slices, optional

- Combine all ingredients and stir well.
- Garnish with orange slices and serve over ice.

Adult Milk Shake

1 cup kahlua
1 pint vanilla ice cream
1 cup half-and-half cream
$\frac{1}{8}$ teaspoon almond extract
$1\frac{2}{3}$ cups crushed ice

- Combine all ingredients in blender and process until smooth.
- Serve immediately.

Lemonade Tea

2 family-size tea bags
$\frac{1}{2}$ cup sugar
1 (12 ounce) can frozen lemonade concentrate
1 quart ginger ale, chilled

- Steep tea in 3 quarts water and mix with sugar and lemonade.
- Add ginger ale just before serving.

Strawberry Crush

2 medium bananas, peeled, sliced
1 pint fresh strawberries, washed, quartered
1 (8 ounce) container strawberry yogurt
$\frac{1}{4}$ cup orange juice

- Place all ingredients in blender and process until smooth.
- Serve as is or over crushed ice.

Pretty People Punch

1 (12 ounce) can frozen limeade concentrate

1 (46 ounce) can pineapple juice, chilled

1 (46 ounce) can apricot nectar, chilled

1 quart ginger ale, chilled

- Dilute limeade concentrate according to can directions.

- Add pineapple juice and apricot nectar and stir well.

- When ready to serve, add ginger ale.

Coffee Surprise

1 tablespoon sugar

4 cups hot, brewed coffee

¾ cup kahlua

Sweetened whipped cream

- Stir sugar into hot coffee and add kahlua.

- Pour into 4 serving cups.

- Top with whipped cream.

Easy Fast
Breakfast
and
Brunch

Food Group Omelet

5 strips bacon, fried, drained, crumbled

⅓ cup sour cream

3 green onions, chopped

1 tablespoon butter

2 eggs

- Combine bacon and sour cream.
- Sauté onions in remaining bacon drippings and add to bacon-sour cream mixture.
- Melt butter in omelet pan.
- Use fork to beat eggs with 1 tablespoon water, pour eggs into omelet pan and cook.
- When omelet is set, spoon sour cream mixture along center and fold omelet onto warm plate.

Fast Cheese Scramble

1 (10 ounce) can cheddar cheese soup

8 eggs, lightly beaten

2 tablespoons (¼ stick) butter

Snipped chives

- Pour soup into bowl and stir until smooth.
- Add eggs and a little pepper and mix well.
- In skillet, melt butter.
- Pour in egg mixture and scramble over low heat until set.
- Sprinkle with chives.

Mexican Scramble

4 tablespoons (½ stick) butter

9 eggs 3 tablespoons milk

5 tablespoons salsa

1 cup crushed tortilla chips

- Melt butter in skillet.
- In bowl, beat eggs and add milk and salsa.
- Pour egg mixture into skillet and stir until eggs are lightly cooked.
- Stir in tortilla chips and serve hot.

Huevos Rancheros

4 corn tortillas

8 eggs

3 tablespoons oil Enchilada sauce

1 cup grated Monterey Jack cheese

- Fry tortillas in hot oil and drain.
- Lightly scramble 2 eggs at a time and place eggs on each tortilla. Repeat process.
- Pour enchilada sauce over eggs.
- Top with cheese and serve with salsa.

Breakfast To-Go

4 eggs
4 flour tortillas
1 cup chopped, cooked ham
1 cup grated cheddar cheese

- Scramble eggs in skillet.
- Lay tortillas flat and spoon eggs over 4 tortillas.
- Sprinkle with ham and cheese and roll up to enclose filling.
- Place tacos in microwave-safe dish and microwave for 30 seconds or until cheese melts.
- Serve immediately.

Breakfast Tortilla Wrap

4 eggs, scrambled
½ cup grated cheddar cheese, divided
½ cup salsa, divided
2 flour tortillas

- For each taco, spread half scrambled eggs, ¼ cup cheese and ¼ cup salsa on tortilla and roll up.

Sugar-Coated Bacon Strips

1 pound bacon
$\frac{1}{3}$ cup packed brown sugar
1 teaspoon flour
$\frac{1}{2}$ cup finely chopped pecans

- Arrange bacon slices close together, but not overlapping, on wire rack over drip pan.
- In bowl, combine brown sugar, flour and pecans and sprinkle evenly over bacon.
- Bake at 350° for 30 minutes. Drain on paper towels.

Sausage Gravy

$\frac{1}{2}$ pound pork sausage
$\frac{1}{4}$ cup flour
$2\frac{1}{2}$ cups milk

- Cook sausage in large skillet over medium heat, stirring until it crumbles. Remove sausage, but reserving about 2 tablespoons drippings in skillet.
- Stir flour into drippings and cook, stirring constantly until flour is slightly brown. Gradually stir in milk and cook, stirring constantly until gravy thickens. Stir in $\frac{3}{4}$ teaspoon black pepper, a little salt and cooked sausages.

Sweet Cherry Oatmeal

2 cups of your favorites cooked oatmeal

½ cup dried cherries, chopped

½ cup packed brown sugar

2 tablespoons butter, softened

½ teaspoon ground cinnamon

½ cup chopped toasted pecans

- While your favorite oatmeal is cooking, combine cherries, brown sugar, butter and cinnamon. Stir into cooked oatmeal.

- Spoon into individual serving bowls and sprinkle toasted pecans over top of each serving.

1-2-3 Omelet

2 tablespoons butter

4–5 eggs

⅓ cup shredded cheddar cheese

- Melt butter in 10-inch skillet over medium heat. While butter melts, whisk together eggs and ¼ teaspoon salt. Pour eggs into skillet and stir gently until they begin to set.

- Spread eggs evenly in pan and sprinkle with cheese. Reduce heat and cook until omelet just sets. Hold skillet over serving plate, tilt skillet until omelet slides out and almost half touches plate. Immediately turn skillet upside down to make omelet fold over itself. Serve immediately.

Zesty French Toast

1 egg, beaten

$^{1}/_{2}$ cup orange juice

5 slices raisin bread

1 cup crushed graham crackers

2 tablespoons butter, more if needed for fyring

- Combine egg and orange juice and dip each slice of bread in egg mixture and then in graham cracker crumbs.

- Fry in batches in butter until light brown.

Gatta Go! Grits

1$^{2}/_{3}$ cups uncooked quick-cooking grits

1 (8 ounce) package shredded sharp cheddar cheese

$^{3}/_{4}$ cup shredded Monterey Jack cheese

$^{2}/_{3}$ cup half-and-half cream

2 tablespoons butter

- In saucepan on medium-high heat, bring 6 cups water, adding a little salt, to a boil and gradually add grits. Reduce heat to low-medium and simmer for 10 minutes, stirring occasionally or until mixture has thickened. Stir in both cheeses, cream and butter, mixing until well blended. Serve immediately.

Sugar and Spice Pears

1 (15 ounce) can pear halves
⅓ cup packed brown sugar
¾ teaspoon ground nutmeg
¾ teaspoon ground cinnamon

- Drain pears, reserve syrup and set pears aside.
- Place syrup, brown sugar, nutmeg and cinnamon in saucepan and bring to a boil.
- Reduce heat and simmer uncovered for 5 to 8 minutes. Stir frequently.
- Add pears and simmer another 5 minutes or until mixture heats through.

Quick Stromboli Bake

1 (10 ounce) tube refrigerated pizza dough
¾ cup shredded cheddar cheese
¾ cup shredded mozzarella cheese
6 bacon strips, cooked, crumbled

- On ungreased baking sheet, roll dough into 12-inch circle.
- On half dough, sprinkle cheeses and bacon to within ½-inch of edge.
- Fold dough over filling and pinch edges to seal.
- Bake at 400° for 10 minutes or until golden brown.
- Cut in pie slices and serve with marinara sauce.

Enchilada Zap

1 dozen corn tortillas

1 (8 ounce) package shredded cheddar cheese, divided

½ cup chopped onion, divided

2 (10 ounce) cans enchilada sauce

- Wrap tortillas in slightly damp paper towel. Place between 2 salad plates and microwave on HIGH for 45 seconds.
- Sprinkle ⅓ cup cheese and some onion on each tortilla and roll up.
- Place seam side down in 9 x 13-inch baking dish. Repeat with remaining tortillas.
- Pour enchilada sauce over tortillas and sprinkle with remaining cheese and onions.
- Cover and microwave on MEDIUM-HIGH for 5 to 6 minutes.

Praline Toast

½ cup (1 stick) butter, softened

1 cup packed brown sugar

½ cup finely chopped pecans Bread slices

- Combine butter, sugar and pecans and mix well.
- Spread on bread slices.
- Toast in broiler until brown and bubbly.

French Toast

4 eggs
1 cup whipping cream
2 thick slices bread, cut into 3 strips
Powdered sugar
Maple syrup

- Place a little oil in skillet.
- Beat eggs, cream and pinch of salt to make batter.
- Dip bread and allow batter to soak in.
- Fry bread in skillet until brown, turn and fry other side. Transfer to baking sheet.
- Bake at 325° for about 4 minutes or until puffed.
- Sprinkle with powdered sugar and serve with maple syrup.

French Toast in Sunshine

1 egg, beaten
½ cup orange juice
5 slices raisin bread
1 cup crushed graham crackers
2 tablespoons butter

- Combine egg and orange juice.
- Dip each slice of bread in egg mixture and then in graham cracker crumbs.
- Fry in butter until brown.

Waffle Ready

2 eggs
1 cup milk
½ teaspoon vanilla extract
8 slices stale bread

- Heat waffle iron according to directions.
- Beat eggs, slowly add milk and vanilla and beat well.
- Remove crust from bread and butter both sides of bread.
- When waffle iron is ready, dip bread in egg mixture and place in waffle iron.
- Close lid and grill until light brown. Serve with syrup.

Island-Flavor Casserole

1 cup sugar
5 tablespoons flour
2 (20 ounce) cans unsweetened pineapple chunks, drained
1½ cups grated cheddar cheese
1 stack round, buttery crackers, crushed
½ cup (1 stick) butter, melted

- Combine sugar and flour.
- Grease 9 x 13-inch baking dish and layer pineapple, sugar-flour mixture, grated cheese and cracker crumbs (in that order).
- Drizzle butter over casserole.
- Bake at 350° for 25 minutes or until bubbly.

This is really a different kind of recipe and very good. It can be served at brunch and is also great with sandwiches at lunch.

Easy Fast Breads

Hot Cheesy Italian Bread

1 (16 ounce) loaf unsliced Italian bread
½ cup refrigerated creamy caesar dressing
⅓ cup grated parmesan cheese
3 tablespoons finely chopped green onions

- Cut 24 (½-inch thick) slices from bread. (Reserve remaining bread for other use.)
- In small bowl, combine dressing, cheese and onion.
- Spread 1 teaspoon dressing mixture on each bread slice.
- Place bread on baking sheet and broil 4 inches from heat until golden brown.
- Serve warm.

Seasoned Bread Bake

1 (16 ounce) loaf unsliced French bread
½ teaspoon garlic powder
1 teaspoon marjoram leaves
1 tablespoon dried parsley leaves
½ cup (1 stick) butter, softened
1 cup parmesan cheese

- Slice bread into 1-inch slices.
- Combine garlic, marjoram, parsley and butter.
- Spread mixture on bread slices and sprinkle with cheese.
- Wrap in foil and bake at 375° for 20 minutes. Unwrap and bake 5 more minutes.

Hot Ranch Loaf

1 (16 ounce) loaf unsliced French bread
½ cup (1 stick) butter, softened
1 tablespoon dry ranch-style salad dressing mix

- Cut loaf in half horizontally.
- Blend butter and dressing mix and spread mixture on bread.
- Wrap bread in foil and bake at 350° for 15 minutes.

English Muffin Tops

½ pound bacon slices, cooked, crumbled
¼ (½ stick) butter, softened
1 (5 ounce) jar sharp processed cheese spread
2 fresh green onion, finely minced

- Preheat oven to 325. In bowl, combine crumbled bacon, butter, cheese and minced onion, mixing well and spread on each half (8) of 4 English muffins.
- Bake for 15 minutes or until each slice is light golden brown.

Veggie Cheese Corn Bread

1 (8 ounce) box corn muffin mix

1 egg

⅓ cup milk

½ cup frozen chopped broccoli, thawed, drained

½ cup cheddar cheese

- Preheat oven to 375°. In bowl, combine muffin mix, egg and milk (the egg and milk are ingredients the mix calls for). Gently stir in chopped broccoli and cheese. (Fresh chopped broccoli or leftover chopped broccoli can also be used.)

- Batter can be placed in muffin pan (with paper cupcake liners) or in greased 8-inch baking pan. If using muffin pan, bake about 18 minutes or 20 to 25 minutes for pan of cornbread.

Presto! Pesto Breadsticks

1 tube (11 ounce) refrigerated breadsticks

¼ cup (½ stick) butter, melted

2 tablespoons prepared pesto

¼ teaspoon garlic powder

3 tablespoons grated parmesan cheese

- Preheat oven to 375°. Unroll and separate breadsticks and place on ungreased baking pan. Combine melted butter, pesto and garlic powder and brush over breadsticks. Twist each breadstick 3 times. Sprinkle with parmesan cheese.

- Bake for about 12 minutes or until golden brown.

Down Home Cornbread

1 cup yellow cornmeal
²⁄₃ cup flour
¹⁄₄ teaspoon baking soda
1¹⁄₄ cups buttermilk
1 large egg, beaten

- Preheat oven to 400°. Combine cornmeal, flour and baking soda in center of bowl and stir in buttermilk and egg, stirring just until moistened.

- Pour into a buttered 7 x 11-inch baking pan and bake 15 minutes or until golden brown.

Garlic Drops

2 teaspoons minced garlic
2 teaspoons dried parsley flakes
2 tablespoons olive oil
¹⁄₂ teaspoon dries oregano
1 (13 ounce) package refrigerated pizza crust

- Preheat oven to 400°. In small bowl, combine garlic, parsley flakes, olive oil and oregano.

- On flat surface, unroll pizza dough and brush with garlic-oil mixture and reroll dough. Using a serrated knife, cut into 1-inch pieces and place each piece in greased muffin pan. Brush any remaining garlic mixture over top of rounds. Bake 15 minutes or until golden brown.

Drop Biscuits

2 cups biscuit mix
⅔ cup milk
⅔ cup grated sharp cheddar cheese
¼ cup (½ stick) butter, melted

- Spray baking sheet with non-stick spray.
- Combine biscuit mix, milk and cheese. Drop 1 heaping tablespoon dough onto baking sheet for each biscuit.
- Bake at 400° for 10 minutes or until light brown.
- While warm, brush tops of biscuits with melted butter. Serve hot.

Green Chile-Cheese Bread

1 (16 ounce) loaf unsliced Italian bread
½ cup (1 stick) butter, melted
1 (4 ounce) can diced green chiles, drained
¾ cup grated Monterey Jack cheese

- Slice bread into 1-inch slices almost all the way through.
- Combine melted butter, chiles and cheese and mix well.
- Spread cheese mixture between bread slices.
- Cover loaf with foil and bake at 350° for 25 minutes.

Cheesy Parmesan Bread

1 (16 ounce) loaf unsliced French bread

12 slices mozzarella cheese

¼ cup grated parmesan cheese

6 tablespoons

(¾ stick) butter, softened

½ teaspoon garlic salt

- Cut loaf into 1-inch thick slices.

- Place mozzarella slices between bread slices.

- Combine parmesan cheese, butter and garlic salt and spread mixture on each slice of bread.

- Reshape loaf, press firmly together and brush remaining butter mixture on outside of loaf.

- Bake at 375° for 8 to 10 minutes.

Easy Creamy Butter Bread

1 cup (2 sticks) butter, softened

2 cups flour

1 (8 ounce) carton sour cream

- Combine all ingredients and mix well.

- Drop by teaspoonfuls into miniature muffin cups.

- Bake at 350° for 20 minutes or until light brown.

Easy Cheese Toast

½ cup (1 stick) butter, softened
1¼ cups shredded cheddar cheese
1 teaspoon Worcestershire sauce
¼ teaspoon garlic powder
Thick-sliced bread

- Combine all ingredients and spread on thick-sliced bread.
- Turn on broiler to preheat. When oven is hot, turn off broiler and put toast in oven for about 15 minutes.

Rosemary's Herb Sticks

1½ teaspoons basil
1 teaspoon rosemary
½ teaspoon thyme
¾ cup (1½ sticks) butter, melted
1 (8 count) package hot dog buns

- Combine basil, rosemary, thyme and butter and let stand several hours at room temperature.
- Spread butter mixture on buns and cut buns into strips.
- Bake at 300° for 15 to 20 minutes or until crisp.

Cheesy Sausage Bites

1 (8 ounce) package grated cheddar cheese
1 pound hot bulk pork sausage
2 cups biscuit mix
¾ cup milk

- Combine cheese, sausage and biscuit mix.
- Drop by teaspoonfuls on ungreased baking sheet.
- Bake at 400° until light brown and serve hot.

Quickie Hot Biscuits

1⅓ cups flour
1 (8 ounce) carton whipping cream
2 tablespoons sugar

- Combine all ingredients and stir until they blend well.
- Drop biscuits by teaspoonfuls onto sprayed baking sheet and bake at 400° for 10 minutes or until light brown.
- Serve with plain or flavored butters.

Garlic-Cheese Biscuits

5 cups biscuit mix
1 cup shredded cheddar cheese
1 (14 ounce) can chicken broth with roasted garlic

- Combine all ingredients to form soft dough.
- Drop by heaping teaspoonfuls onto sprayed baking sheet.
- Bake at 425° for 10 minutes or until light brown.

French Onion Biscuits

2 cups biscuit mix
¼ cup milk
1 (8 ounce) container French onion dip
2 tablespoons finely minced green onion

- Mix all ingredients until soft dough forms.
- Drop dough by teaspoonfuls onto sprayed baking sheet.
- Bake at 400° for 10 minutes or until light brown.

Hot Creamy Butter Biscuits

1 (3 ounce) package cream cheese, softened
$\frac{1}{2}$ cup (1 stick) butter, softened
1 cup flour
$\frac{1}{4}$ teaspoon salt, optional

- Use mixer to beat cream cheese and butter.
- Add flour and mix well.
- Roll out dough to $\frac{1}{2}$-inch thickness and cut out biscuits with small biscuit cutter.
- Place on greased baking sheet and bake at 350° for 20 minutes or until light brown.

Fast Biscuit Bake

$\frac{1}{3}$ cup club soda
$\frac{1}{3}$ cup sour cream
$\frac{1}{2}$ tablespoon sugar
2 cups biscuit mix

- In mixing bowl, combine all ingredients with fork just until dry ingredients are moist.
- Turn bowl out onto lightly floured board and knead gently several times.
- Roll dough to 1-inch thickness and cut out biscuits with biscuit cutter.
- Place dough in sprayed 9 x 13-inch baking pan.
- Bake at 400° for 12 to14 minutes or until golden brown.

Lickety-Split Biscuits

2 cups self-rising flour
4 tablespoons mayonnaise
1 cup milk

- Mix all ingredients and drop by teaspoonfuls on baking sheet.
- Bake at 425° until biscuits are golden brown.

Miss Sadie's Sweet Potato Biscuits

1 (16 ounce) can sweet potatoes, drained
1 tablespoon sugar
¼ cup milk
1½ cups biscuit mix

- In mixing bowl, mash sweet potatoes, add sugar and milk and beat until creamy.
- Stir in biscuit mix with fork until most lumps are gone.
- Pour mixture onto floured wax paper and knead 5 to 6 times.
- Press down to about ½-inch thick and cut out biscuits with biscuit cutter or small glass.
- Bake at 450° for 10 to 12 minutes on ungreased baking sheet.

Mammy's Old-Time Biscuits

2¼ cups biscuit mix
⅔ cup milk
1½ cups maple syrup

- Combine biscuit mix and milk and stir just until moist.
- On floured surface, roll dough to ½-inch thickness. Cut out biscuits with 2-inch biscuit cutter.
- Pour syrup into 7 x 11-inch baking dish. Place biscuits on top of syrup.
- Bake at 425° for 13 to 15 minutes or until biscuits are golden brown.

Date Biscuits

1 cup chopped dates
2 cups biscuit mix
½ cup grated American cheese
¾ cup milk

- Combine dates, biscuit mix and cheese.
- Add milk and stir well into moderately soft dough.
- Drop by teaspoonfuls onto sprayed baking sheet.
- Bake at 400° for 12 to 15 minutes and serve hot.

Get 'Em Hot Biscuits

2 cups flour
4 tablespoons mayonnaise
1 cup milk

- Combine all ingredients and drop by teaspoonfuls on baking sheet.
- Bake at 425° until biscuits are golden brown.
- Serve with plain or flavored butters.

Corny Dinner Sticks

2 cups biscuit mix
1 (8 ounce) can cream-style corn
2 tablespoons minced green onion Melted butter

- Combine biscuit mix, cream-style corn and green onions.
- Place dough on floured surface and cut into 3 x 1-inch strips. Roll strips in melted butter.
- Bake at 400° for 15 minutes.

Spicy Cornbread Twists

3 tablespoons butter
⅓ cup cornmeal
¼ teaspoon red pepper
1 (11 ounce) can refrigerated soft breadsticks

- Place butter in pie plate and melt in oven. Remove from oven.
- On wax paper, mix cornmeal and red pepper.
- Roll breadsticks in butter and in cornmeal mixture.
- Twist breadsticks according to package directions and place on cookie sheet.
- Bake at 350° for 15 to 18 minutes.

Cream-Style Cornbread

1 cup self-rising cornmeal
1 (8 ounce) can cream-style corn
1 (8 ounce) carton sour cream
3 large eggs, lightly beaten
¼ cup oil

- Heat lightly greased 8-inch cast-iron skillet in oven at 400°.
- Combine all ingredients and stir just until moist.
- Remove prepared skillet from oven and spoon batter into hot skillet.
- Bake at 400° for 20 minutes or until golden.

Quick Scratch Muffins

1 (16 ounce) package blueberry muffin mix with
blueberries

2 egg whites

½ cup orange juice

Orange marmalade

- Wash blueberries with cold water and drain.

- Stir muffin mix, egg whites and orange juice and break
up any lumps.

- Fold blueberries gently into batter and pour into muffin
tins (with paper liners) about half full.

- Bake at 370° for 18 to 20 minutes or until toothpick
inserted in center comes out clean.

- Spoon orange marmalade over top of hot muffins.

Gingerbread Muffins

1 (16 ounce) box gingerbread mix

1¼ cups lukewarm water

1 egg

2 (1.5 ounce) boxes seedless raisins

- Combine gingerbread mix, water and egg and mix well.
Stir in raisins.

- Pour into sprayed muffin tins and fill half full.

- Bake at 350° for 20 minutes or when tested done with
toothpick.

Sweet Cake Poppers

1 cup flour
1 cup whipping cream
2 tablespoons sugar
$\frac{1}{8}$ teaspoon ground cinnamon

- Combine all ingredients and pour into greased mini-muffin cups.
- Bake at 375° for 10 to 15 minutes.

Homemade Rolls

2 cups biscuit mix
1 (8 ounce) carton sour cream
$\frac{1}{2}$ cup (1 stick) butter, melted

- Combine all ingredients and mix well. Spoon into greased muffin tins and fill only half full.
- Bake at 400° for 12 to 14 minutes or until rolls are light brown.

Beer Biscuits

3¼ cups biscuit mix

¼ teaspoon salt

1 teaspoon sugar

1⅔ cups beer

- Combine all ingredients and spoon into 12 sprayed muffin cups.

- Bake at 400° for 15 to 20 minutes or until biscuits are golden brown.

Mayo Muffins

1¼ cups flour

3 tablespoons mayonnaise

1 cup whole milk

- Combine all ingredients and spoon into sprayed muffin tins.

- Bake at 375° for 20 minutes or until muffins are light brown.

Easy Fast Soups

Swiss-Family Soup

1 (1 ounce) package dry vegetable soup mix

3 cups water 1 cup half-and-half cream

1 ½ cups shredded Swiss cheese

- Combine soup mix and water in saucepan and bring to boil.
- Lower heat and simmer for 10 minutes.
- Add half-and-half and cheese and serve hot.

Creamy Broccoli-Rice Soup

This is a hearty and delicious soup that is full of flavor.

1 (6 ounce) package chicken-flavored wild rice mix

1 (10 ounce) package frozen chopped broccoli, thawed

2 teaspoons dried minced onion

1 (10 ounce) can cream of chicken soup

1 (8 ounce) package cream cheese, cubed

- In large saucepan, combine rice, rice seasoning packet and 6 cups water.
- Bring to a boil, reduce heat, cover and simmer for 10 minutes, stirring once.
- Stir in broccoli and onion and simmer 5 minutes.
- Stir in soup and cream cheese.
- Cook and stir until cheese melts.

Cream of Zucchini Soup

1 pound fresh zucchini, grated
1 onion, chopped
1 (14 ounce) can chicken broth
½ teaspoon sweet basil
2 cups half-and-half cream, divided

- In saucepan, combine zucchini, onion, broth, basil and a little salt and pepper.
- Bring to a boil, simmer until soft, pour into food processor and purée.
- Gradually add ½ cup cream and blend. (You could add ¼ teaspoon curry powder if you like curry flavor.)
- Return zucchini mixture to saucepan and add remaining cream. Heat but do not boil.

Harvest-Time Butternut Soup

4 cups cooked, mashed butternut squash
2 (14 ounce) cans chicken broth
½ teaspoon sugar
1 (8 ounce) carton whipping cream, divided
¼ teaspoon ground nutmeg

- In saucepan, combine mashed squash, broth, sugar and a little salt.
- Bring to a boil, gradually stir in half of whipping cream and cook until thoroughly heated.
- Beat remaining whipping cream and, when ready to serve, place dollop of whipped cream on soup and sprinkle with nutmeg.

Fast Ham-Bean Soup

3 (16 ounce) cans navy beans with liquid

1 (14 ounce) can chicken broth

1 cup chopped ham 1 large onion, chopped

$\frac{1}{2}$ teaspoon garlic powder

- In large saucepan, combine all ingredients, add 1 cup water and bring to a boil.
- Simmer until onion is tender-crisp and serve hot with cornbread.

Sippin' Peanut Butter Soup

2 (10 ounce) cans cream of chicken soup

2 soup cans milk

$1\frac{1}{4}$ cups crunchy-style peanut butter

- In saucepan on medium heat, blend soup and milk.
- Stir in peanut butter and heat until well blended.

Super Fast Gumbo

1 (10 ounce) can condensed pepper pot soup

1 (10 ounce) can condensed chicken-gumbo soup

1 (6 ounce) can white crabmeat, flaked

1 (6 ounce) can tiny, cooked shrimp

- Combine all ingredients with $1\frac{1}{2}$ soup cans water.
- Cover and simmer for 15 minutes.

Cold Cucumber Soup

3 medium cucumbers, peeled, seeded, cut into chunks

1 (14 ounce) can chicken broth, divided

1 (8 ounce) carton sour cream

3 tablespoons fresh chives, minced

2 teaspoon fresh dill, minced

- In blender, combine cucumbers, 1 cup chicken broth and a dash of salt, cover and process until smooth.
- Transfer cucumber mixture to medium bowl and stir in remaining chicken broth.
- Whisk in sour cream, chives and dill, cover and chill well before serving.
- Garnish with dill sprig.

Chowder Blend

1 (10 ounce) can New England clam chowder

1 (10 ounce) can cream of celery soup

1 (10 ounce) can cream of potato soup

1 (6 ounce) can chopped clams

1 (10 ounce) soup can milk

- Combine all ingredients in saucepan.
- Heat and stir.

Arriba Taco Soup

1 (12 ounce) can chicken with liquid
1 (14 ounce) can chicken broth
1 (16 ounce) jar mild thick and chunky salsa
1 (15 ounce) can ranch-style beans

● In large saucepan, combine all ingredients.
● Bring to a boil, reduce heat and simmer for 15 minutes.

Easy Fast
Salads

Mixed Salad Crunch

6 cups torn mixed salad greens
1 medium zucchini, sliced
1 (8 ounce) can sliced water chestnuts, drained
½ cup peanuts
⅓ cup Italian salad dressing

- Toss greens, zucchini, water chestnuts and peanuts.
- When ready to serve, add salad dressing and toss.

Strawberry-Banana Surprise

1 (10 ounce) bag fresh spinach, washed, stemmed
1 pint fresh strawberries, stemmed, halved
1 large banana, sliced
⅔ cup chopped walnuts

- Combine all salad ingredients in large bowl.
- When ready to serve, toss with prepared salad dressing.

Christmas Salad

4 cups torn mixed salad greens
3 fresh green onions with tops, chopped
2 medium red apples with peel, diced
1 cup fresh raspberries
½ cup prepared poppy seed dressing

- In bowl, toss salad greens, onions and fruit.
- Drizzle with dressing and toss.

Mixed Mandarin Salad

1 head red-tipped lettuce
2 (11 ounce) cans mandarin oranges, drained
2 avocados, peeled, diced
1 small red onion, sliced

- Combine all ingredients.
- When ready to serve, toss with prepared poppy seed salad dressing.

Grapefruit-Avocado Salad

2 (15 ounce) cans grapefruit sections, drained
2 ripe avocados, peeled, sliced
½ cup chopped slivered almonds
Prepared poppy seed salad dressing

- Combine grapefruit, avocados and almonds.
- Toss with dressing.
- Serve on bed of lettuce.

Warm Spinach Salad

1 (8 ounce) package fresh spinach

3 hard-boiled eggs, chopped

8 mushroom caps, sliced

1 (8 ounce) can sliced water chestnuts, drained

- Combine all ingredients and serve with Hot Bacon Dressing.

Hot Bacon Dressing:

½ pound bacon, chopped

1 cup sugar

1⅓ cups white vinegar

5 teaspoons cornstarch

- Fry bacon until crisp, drain and leave bacon drippings in skillet.

- Add sugar and vinegar to skillet and stir well.

- Add 1 cup water and bring to a boil.

- Mix cornstarch with ⅔ cup water, stir until it dissolves and pour cornstarch mixture into skillet with dressing.

- Return to boil and simmer for 5 minutes.

- Remove from heat, return bacon to skillet and toss dressing into salad.

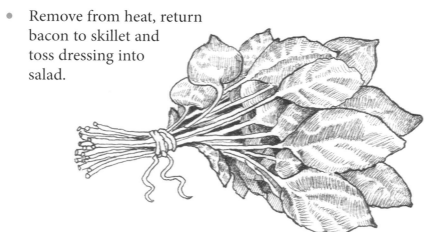

Easy Guacamole Salad

4 avocados, softened
1 (8 ounce) package cream cheese, softened
1 (10 ounce) can diced tomatoes and green chiles
1½ teaspoons garlic salt
About 1 tablespoon lemon juice

- Peel avocados and mash with fork.
- In mixing bowl, beat cream cheese until smooth, add avocados, tomatoes and green chiles, garlic salt and lemon juice and mix well.
- Serve on lettuce leaf with a few tortilla chips beside salad.

Green Pea-Cauliflower Salad

1 (16 ounce) package frozen green peas, thawed, uncooked
1 head cauliflower, cut into florets
1 (8 ounce) carton sour cream
1 (1 ounce) package dry ranch-style salad dressing mix

- In large bowl, combine peas and cauliflower.
- Combine sour cream and salad dressing, toss with vegetables and chill.

Butter Bean-Corn Salad

2 (10 ounce) packages frozen baby limas
1 (15 ounce) can shoe-peg corn, drained
1 bunch fresh green onions with tops, chopped
1 cup mayonnaise
2 teaspoons dry ranch-style salad dressing mix

- Cook beans according to package directions and drain.
- Add corn, onions, mayonnaise and dressing mix, combine well and chill.

Crunchy Pea Salad

1 (16 ounce) package frozen green peas, thawed
$\frac{1}{4}$ cup diced celery
1 bunch fresh green onions with tops, chopped
1 cup chopped cashews
$\frac{1}{2}$ cup mayonnaise

- Combine peas, celery, onions and cashews.
- Toss with mayonnaise seasoned with $\frac{1}{2}$ teaspoon seasoned salt and black pepper.

Flavorific Rice Salad

This rice salad has lots of flavor!

1 (6 ounce) package chicken-flavored rice and macaroni
¾ cup chopped green pepper
1 bunch fresh green onion with tops, chopped
2 (6 ounce) jars marinated artichoke hearts
½ to ⅔ cup mayonnaise

- Cook rice and macaroni according to directions (but without butter), drain and cool.
- Add green pepper, onions, artichoke hearts and mayonnaise, toss and chill.

Rainbow Salad

1 (16 ounce) package tri-colored macaroni, cooked, drained
1 red bell pepper, cut into julienne strips
1 cup chopped zucchini
1 cup broccoli florets
Caesar salad dressing

- Combine all ingredients.
- Toss with 1 cup caesar salad dressing and chill.

Really Good Noodle Salad

1 cup slivered almonds
1 cup sunflower seeds
2 (3 ounce) packages chicken-flavored ramen noodles
1 (16 ounce) package broccoli slaw
1 (8 ounce) bottle Italian salad dressing

- Toast almonds and sunflower seeds in oven at 275° for about 10 minutes.
- Break up ramen noodles (discard seasoning packets) and mix with slaw, almonds and sunflower seeds.
- Toss with Italian salad dressing and chill.

Little Apple Annie Salad

2 apples, cored, chopped
1 cup seedless green grapes, halved
$\frac{1}{2}$ cup chopped celery
$\frac{3}{4}$ cup chopped pecans
$\frac{1}{3}$ cup mayonnaise

- Combine all ingredients and chill.

Easy Creamy Slaw

1 medium green cabbage, shredded

½ onion, chopped

⅓ cup sugar

1 cup mayonnaise

¼ cup vinegar

- Toss cabbage and onion together, add salt and pepper to taste and sprinkle sugar over mixture.
- Combine mayonnaise and vinegar and pour over cabbage and onion.
- Toss and chill.

Fruit Fandango Salad

2 (11 ounce) cans mandarin oranges

2 (15 ounce) cans pineapple chunks

1 (16 ounce) carton frozen strawberries, thawed

1 (20 ounce) can peach pie filling

1 (20 ounce) can apricot pie filling

- Drain oranges, pineapple and strawberries.
- Combine all ingredients and fold together gently.

Kids' Favorite Salad

6 large apples with peel, chopped
6 (2 ounce) Snicker candy bars, chopped
½ cup chopped pecans, optional
1 (12 ounce) carton whipped topping

- In large bowl, combine apples, candy bars and pecans and mix well.
- Fold in whipped topping and chill.

Fruit Fluff

2 (20 ounce) cans pineapple tidbits, drained
1 (16 ounce) can whole cranberry sauce
2 (11 ounce) cans mandarin oranges, drained
½ cup chopped pecans
1 (8 ounce) carton whipped topping

- In bowl, combine pineapple, cranberry sauce, oranges, and pecans and fold in whipped topping.
- Serve in pretty crystal bowl.

Orange-Mandarin Fluff

1 (16 ounce) carton small-curd cottage cheese

1 (6 ounce) package orange gelatin

2 (11 ounce) cans mandarin oranges, drained

1 (20 ounce) can chunk pineapple, drained

1 (8 ounce) carton whipped topping

- Sprinkle gelatin over cottage cheese and mix well.
- Add oranges and pineapple and mix well.
- Fold in whipped topping, chill, and serve in pretty crystal bowl.

Quickie Chicken Salad

3 cups chicken breast halves, cooked, finely chopped

1½ cups chopped celery

½ cup sweet pickle relish

2 hard-boiled eggs, chopped

¾ cup mayonnaise

- Combine all ingredients and several sprinkles salt and pepper.

Adding ½ cup chopped pecans gives the chicken salad a special taste.

Chicken Strip Mix

4 boneless, skinless chicken breast halves, cooked
1 cup chopped celery
1 red bell pepper, seeded, chopped
⅔ cup slivered almonds, toasted

- Slice chicken breasts into long, thin strips.
- Combine chicken, celery, bell pepper and almonds.
- Toss and chill.

For dressing use flavored mayonnaise: ½ cup mayonnaise with 1 tablespoon lemon juice.

Easy Broccoli-Chicken Fest

3 to 4 boneless, skinless chicken breast halves, cooked, cubed
2 cups fresh broccoli florets
1 sweet red bell pepper, seeded, chopped
1 cup chopped celery

- Combine all ingredients.
- Toss mixture with honey-mustard salad dressing and chill.

Tarragon-Chicken Salad

1 cup chopped pecans

3 to 4 boneless, skinless chicken breast halves, cooked, cubed

1 cup chopped celery

¾ cup peeled, chopped cucumbers

- Place pecans in shallow pan and toast at 300° for 10 minutes.
- Combine chicken, celery and cucumbers.

Dressing for Tarragon-Chicken Salad:

⅔ cup mayonnaise

1 tablespoon lemon juice

2 tablespoons tarragon vinegar

1¼ teaspoons crumbled, dried tarragon

- Combine all dressing ingredients and mix well.
- When ready to serve, toss with chicken mixture and add pecans.

Easy Fast
Sandwiches

Saturday Night Sandwiches

1 (8 ounce) package cream cheese, softened
⅓ cup chopped stuffed olives
2 tablespoons olive juice
⅓ cup chopped pecans
6 slices bacon, cooked, crumbled

- Beat cream cheese with mixer until smooth and stir in olives, olive juice, pecans and bacon.
- Spread on party rye bread.

Sunny-Side-Up Turkey Sandwiches

4 (1 ounce) slices cheddar cheese
2 English muffins, split, toasted
½ pound thinly sliced turkey
1 (15 ounce) can asparagus spears, drained
1 (1 ounce) package hollandaise sauce blend

- Place 1 cheese slice on each muffin half and top evenly with turkey.
- Cut asparagus spears to fit muffin halves and top each with 3 or 4 asparagus spears. (Reserve remaining asparagus for another use.)
- Prepare sauce mix according to package directions, pour evenly over sandwiches and sprinkle with paprika, if desired.

Celebration Sandwiches

1 tablespoon lemon juice
1 (8 ounce) package cream cheese, softened Mayonnaise
½ cup grated carrots
¼ cup each grated cucumber, purple onion and bell pepper

- Combine lemon juice with cream cheese and add enough mayonnaise to make cheese into spreading consistency.
- Fold in grated vegetables, spread on bread for sandwiches and chill.

Happy Reuben Broils

For each sandwich:
2 slices rye bread
1 slice Swiss cheese
Generous slices corned beef
2 tablespoons sauerkraut Dijon mustard

- Butter 1 slice bread on 1 side and place butter side down in skillet over low heat.
- Layer cheese, corned beef and sauerkraut on bread.
- Spread mustard on 1 side of other slice, butter opposite side of bread and place butter side up on sauerkraut.
- Cook until bottom browns, turn carefully and brown other side.

Kids' Special Snacks

Peanut butter
8 slices English muffins
2 bananas
8 slices bacon, cooked crispy
Butter, softened

- Spread peanut butter over 8 slices of muffin.
- Slice bananas and arrange on top of 4 muffin halves.
- Place 2 strips bacon on each of 4 muffin halves on top of banana slices.
- Top with remaining muffin slices and spread butter over top slice.
- Brown sandwiches butter side down.
- Spread butter other side, turn and cook until golden brown. Serve hot.

Lightning Pizza

1 (14 ounce) package English muffins
1½ cups pizza sauce
1 pound bulk sausage, cooked, drained
1 (4 ounce) can mushrooms, drained
1 (8 ounce) package shredded mozzarella cheese

- Split muffins and layer ingredients on each muffin half ending with cheese.
- Broil until cheese melts.

Ham and Cheese Hot Pockets

1 (8 ounce) can refrigerated crescent rolls
2 tablespoons mayonnaise
2 teaspoons prepared mustard
1 cup finely chopped ham
$\frac{1}{2}$ cup shredded Swiss cheese

- Unroll dough, separate into 4 rectangles and press seams to seal.
- Combine mayonnaise and mustard and spread over rectangles, leaving a $\frac{1}{2}$ inch border.
- Sprinkle ham and cheese evenly over half of each rectangle.
- Moisten edges with water, fold dough over and pinch edges to seal.
- Bake at 375° for 10 minutes or until puffed and golden.

Long Reubens

1 (1 pound) package smoked frankfurter
8 hot dog buns
1 (8 ounce) can sauerkraut, well drained
Caraway seeds

- Preheat oven to 325°.
- Pierce each frankfurter and place into split buns.
- Arrange 2 tablespoons sauerkraut over each frank and sprinkle with caraway seeds.
- Place in 9 x 13-inch shallow pan and drizzle with thousand island salad dressing.
- Heat 10 minutes or just until franks are thoroughly hot.

Everyday Sloppy Joes

1 pound lean ground beef
1 (10 ounce) can Italian tomato soup
2 teaspoons Worcestershire sauce
⅛ teaspoon black pepper
6 hamburger buns, split, toasted

- In skillet, cook beef until brown, stir to separate meat and spoon off fat.
- Add soup, Worcestershire, pepper and ¼ cup water.
- Heat thoroughly and stir often.
- Serve on buns.

Hot Meatball Hoagies

1 small onion, diced
1 small green bell pepper, diced
1 (15 ounce) can sloppy joe sauce
30 to 32 frozen cooked meatballs
4 hoagie buns

- Sauté onion and pepper in 1 tablespoon oil.
- Add sauce and meatballs and cook 10 minutes or until thoroughly heated, stirring often.
- Spoon evenly onto hoagie buns.

Easy Cheesy Wiener Dogs

8 wieners

8 slices cheese

1 (8 ounce) package refrigerated crescent rolls

- Split wieners lengthwise and fill with folded cheese slice.
- Wrap wiener in crescent dough roll and bake at 375° for 12 minutes.
- Serve with mustard.

Tuesday's Turkey Day

1 (8 ounce) package cream cheese, softened

¼ cup orange marmalade

6 large croissants, split

Lettuce leaves

1 pound thinly sliced, cooked turkey

¾ cup whole cranberry sauce

- Beat cream cheese and orange marmalade and spread evenly on cut sides of croissants.
- Place lettuce leaves and turkey on croissant bottoms and spread with cranberry sauce.
- Cover with croissant tops.

Reuben Dogs

1 (20 ounce) can sauerkraut, rinsed, drained
2 teaspoons caraway seeds
8 hot dogs, halved lengthwise
1 cup shredded Swiss cheese
Thousand Island salad dressing

- Place sauerkraut in greased 2-quart baking dish, sprinkle with caraway seeds and top with hot dogs.
- Bake uncovered at 350° for 20 minutes or until heated through.
- Sprinkle with cheese and bake 3 to 5 minutes longer or until cheese melts.
- Serve with salad dressing.

15-Minute Lunch Rolls

8 large wieners
4 slices American cheese, cut into 6 strips each
1 (8 ounce) can refrigerated crescent dinner rolls

- Slit wieners to within ½-inch of end and insert 3 strips cheese in each slit.
- Separate crescent dough into 8 triangles and wrap dough around wiener.
- Keep cheese side up and place on baking sheet.
- Bake at 375° for 12 to 15 minutes or until golden brown.

Sandwiches Extraordinaire

Here are some new or different combinations for sandwiches you may not have tried before. You'll get some "ooh"s and "aah"s and maybe even a raised eyebrow or two.

Deli Delight

Hoagie Rolls
Dijon-style mustard
Slices of pastrami
Slices of mozzarella cheese
Deli coleslaw

California Rye-Guy

Rye bread
mozzarella cheese
Deli ham salad
Avocado slices
Lettuce

Seafood Dissapear

Whole wheat bread
Slices of American cheese
Deli shrimp or crab salad
Avocado slices
Lettuce

Creamy Egg Salad Sandwich

Kaiser Rolls
Spread with softened cream cheese
Deli egg salad
Slices of dill pickles
Fresh bean sprouts

Sandwich Spreads

Just combine all the ingredients and refrigerate.

Horseradish Mayonnaise:

$\frac{1}{2}$ cup mayonnaise

1 tablespoon chopped fresh chives

1 tablespoon prepared horseradish

$\frac{1}{8}$ teaspoon seasoned salt

Garlic Mayonnaise:

$\frac{2}{3}$ cup mayonnaise

1 tablespoon chopped roasted garlic

1 teaspoon finely chopped onion

$\frac{1}{8}$ teaspoon salt

Sesame-Ginger Mayonnaise:

$\frac{2}{3}$ cup mayonnaise

1 tablespoon honey

1 tablespoon toasted sesame seeds

2 teaspoon grated fresh ginger root

Quick Guacamole:

1 (1 ounce) package dry onion soup mix

2 (8 ounce) cartons avocado dip

2 green onions with tops, chopped

$\frac{1}{2}$ teaspoon crushed dillweed

Bridge Club Sandwiches

2 (8 ounce) packages cream cheese, softened
1 (4 ounce) can black olives, chopped
¾ cups finely chopped pecans
Pumpernickel rye bread

- Beat cream cheese until creamy and fold in olives and pecans.
- Trim crusts from bread and spread cream cheese on bread.
- Slice sandwich into 3 finger strips.

Philly's Competition Burger

⅓ cup finely cubed provolone cheese
¼ cup diced roasted red peppers
¼ cup finely chopped onion
1 pound lean ground beef
4 hamburger buns, split

- In bowl, combine cheese, red peppers, onion and a little salt and pepper.
- Add beef, mix well and shape into 4 patties.
- Grill covered over medium-hot heat for 5 minutes on each side or until meat is no longer pink.
- Add your favorite lettuce, tomatoes, etc. and serve on hamburger buns.

Burger with Flair

Basic Burger

1¼ pounds ground chuck

1 egg, optional

2 teaspoons Worcestershire sauce

½ teaspoon salt

¼ teaspoon black pepper

- Mix ground chuck with egg, Worcestershire, salt and pepper.
- Form into 4 or 5 patties about ½-inch thick and about 4 inches in diameter.
- Cook on grill for about 5 to 6 minutes on each side or in skillet for about 4 to 5 minutes on each side.
- Toast 4 buns and spread with mayonnaise or mustard.
- Add lettuce, tomatoes and slice of onion and serve.

Here are some suggested additions to your basic hamburger for a little change of taste:

Tex-Mex Burgers:

- Spread some prepared guacamole and place sliced jalapeno peppers on each bun.

Garden Burgers:

- Instead of lettuce, place about 3 tablespoons deli-prepared coleslaw and some sunflower seeds on each bun.

Nutty Harvest Burgers:

- Add thin slices of apples and some chopped peanuts.

Farmer-In-The-Dell Burgers:

- Add thin slices of cucumber and sliced olives.

South-Of-The-Border Burger:

- Instead of American cheese, use Monterey Jack cheese, and instead of mayonnaise or mustard, use prepared guacamole as spread.

Pastrami-Cheese Burgers:

- Add slices of pastrami and slices of mozzarella cheese.

Salami-Swiss Burgers:

- Add slices of salami and slices of Swiss cheese.

Bacon-Mex Burgers:

- Add slices of avocado, mayonnaise (not mustard) and slices of crisp, cooked bacon.

Cheeseburger Melt

1 (1 ounce) package dry ranch-style salad dressing mix
1 pound lean ground beef
1 cup shredded cheddar cheese
4 large hamburger buns, toasted

- Combine dressing mix with beef and cheese.
- Shape into 4 patties, cook covered on grill until patties are brown and fully done.

Pizza Burger

1 pound lean ground beef
½ teaspoon salt
½ cup pizza sauce, divided
4 slices mozzarella cheese

- Combine beef, salt and half pizza sauce.
- Mold into 4 patties and pan-fry over medium heat for 5 to 6 minutes on each side.
- Just before burgers are done, top each with 1 spoonful pizza sauce and 1 slice cheese.
- Serve on hamburger buns.

Frankly Tacos

1 (10 ounce) can chili hot dog sauce
1 (10 count) package beef franks
1 (10 count) package pre-formed taco shells Shredded cheddar cheese

- Place chili sauce in saucepan and heat to warm.
- Place 1 frank in each taco shell and top with warm chili sauce and cheese. (Add onions and tomatoes if you like.)
- Place in microwave and heat for 30 seconds or until frankfurters warm.

Easy Fast
Side Dishes

Mashed Potatoes Round-Up

4 cups prepared, unsalted instant mashed potatoes
1 (1 ounce) package ranch-style salad dressing mix
¼ cup (½ stick) butter
½ cup sour cream

- Combine all ingredients in saucepan and mix well.
- Heat on low until potatoes are thoroughly heated.

Potatoes Au Gratin

5 to 6 medium potatoes
1 (8 ounce) carton sour cream
1 (1 ounce) package dry ranch-style salad dressing mix
1½ cups shredded cheddar cheese
3 pieces bacon, fried, drained, crumbled or real bacon bits

- Peel, slice and boil potatoes and drain.
- Place potatoes in 2-quart baking dish.
- Combine sour cream, salad dressing mix and a little pepper.
- Toss until potatoes are coated with sour cream mixture and sprinkle cheese on top.
- Bake at 350° for about 20 minutes.
- Sprinkle bacon on top and serve hot.

Double-Cheesy Potatoes

6 to 8 baked potatoes

1 (8 ounce) carton sour cream

1 (8 ounce) package cream cheese, softened

1 ½ cups shredded cheddar cheese

- Cut potatoes in half lengthwise, scoop meat from potatoes and place meat in mixing bowl.

- Add sour cream, cream cheese and salt to taste and whip until all blend.

- Spoon mashed potatoes back into potato skins and place in oven until potatoes reheat.

- Sprinkle cheddar cheese over potatoes.

Potato Hotcakes

3 pounds white potatoes, peeled, grated

1 onion, finely minced

3 eggs, beaten

½ cup dry seasoned breadcrumbs

- In large bowl, combine potatoes, onion, eggs, breadcrumbs and a little salt and pepper and mix well.

- Drop mixture by spoonfuls into skillet with hot oil and brown on both sides.

Broccoli-Cheese Potatoes

4 hot baked potatoes, halved
1 cup diced, cooked ham
1 (10 ounce) can cream of broccoli soup
½ cup shredded cheddar cheese

- Place hot baked potatoes in microwave-safe dish.
- Carefully fluff up potatoes with fork and top each potato with ham.
- Stir soup in can until smooth and spoon over potatoes.
- Top with cheese and microwave on HIGH for 4 minutes.

New-Italy Potatoes

1½ pounds new potatoes
6 tablespoons (¾ stick) butter, sliced
¼ teaspoon thyme
½ cup chopped fresh parsley
½ teaspoon rosemary

- Scrub potatoes and cut in halves but do not peel.
- In medium saucepan, boil potatoes in lightly salted water for about 20 minutes or until tender and drain.
- Add butter, thyme, parsley and rosemary and toss gently until butter melts.
- Serve hot.

Sweet-Sweet Tater Casserole

1 (28 ounce) can sweet potatoes
½ cup chopped pecans
1½ cups packed light brown sugar
½ cup (1 stick) butter

- Slice sweet potatoes into 2-quart casserole dish and sprinkle with pecans.
- Combine brown sugar and butter with just enough water to make syrup and bring mixture to a boil.
- Pour syrup over sweet potatoes and bake at 350° for 30 minutes until potatoes brown.

Thanksgiving in July Potatoes

2 (15 ounce) cans sweet potatoes
¼ cup (½ stick) butter, melted
¼ cup orange juice
1 cup miniature marshmallows

- Combine sweet potatoes, butter, orange juice and ½ teaspoon salt in mixing bowl.
- Beat until fluffy and fold in marshmallows.
- Spoon mixture into buttered 2-quart casserole dish.
- Bake uncovered at 350° for 25 minutes.

You might want to sprinkle top with additional marshmallows and broil until light brown.

Swift 'n Sweet Potatoes

2 (16 ounce) cans sweet potatoes, drained
1 (8 ounce) can crushed pineapple with juice
½ cup chopped pecans
⅓ cup packed brown sugar
1 cup miniature marshmallows, divided

- In 2-quart microwave-safe dish, layer sweet potatoes, a little salt, pineapple, pecans, brown sugar and ½ cup marshmallows.
- Cover and microwave on HIGH for 6 minutes or until bubbly around edges.
- Top with remaining marshmallows and heat uncovered on HIGH for 30 seconds or until marshmallows puff. (If you like, sprinkle sweet potatoes with a little nutmeg.)

Spinach Fettuccine

1 (6 ounce) can tomato paste
1 (5 ounce) can evaporated milk
½ cup (1 stick) butter
1 (12 ounce) package spinach fettuccine

- Cook fettuccine according to package directions.
- In saucepan, combine tomato paste, milk and butter and heat until butter melts.
- Season with a little salt and pepper.
- Serve sauce over fettuccine.

Easy-Creamy Pasta

4 ounces spinach linguine, uncooked

1 cup whipping cream

1 cup chicken broth

½ cup freshly grated parmesan cheese

½ cup frozen English peas

- Cook linguine according to package directions, drain and keep warm.

- Combine whipping cream and chicken broth in saucepan and bring to boil.

- Reduce heat and simmer mixture 25 minutes or until it thickens and reduces to 1 cup.

- Remove from heat, add cheese and peas and stir until cheese melts.

- Toss with linguine and serve immediately.

Sausage Fettuccine

1 (8 ounce) package fettuccine

1 pound Italian sausage

1 (10 ounce) can cream of mushroom soup

1 (16 ounce) carton sour cream

- Cook fettuccine according to package directions and drain.

- Cut sausage into 1-inch pieces, brown over medium heat, cook for 8 minutes and drain.

- Combine all ingredients and pour into 2-quart greased baking dish.

- Bake at 325° for 30 minutes.

Presto Pasta

2½ cups uncooked small tube pasta
1 small onion, chopped
2 tablespoons oil
2½ tablespoons dried basil
1 cup shredded mozzarella cheese

- Cook pasta according to package directions.
- In skillet, sauté onion in oil.
- Stir in basil, 1 teaspoon salt and ¼ teaspoon pepper, cook and stir 1 minute.
- Drain pasta and add to basil mixture. (Leave about ½ cup water so pasta won't be too dry.)
- Remove from heat and stir in cheese just until it begins to melt.
- Serve immediately.

OOOO-eee Rice

1 (16 ounce) package smoked sausage, sliced
2 (10 ounce) cans diced tomato and green chiles
3 cups chicken broth
2 teaspoons Creole seasoning
1½ cups uncooked, long-grain rice

- Sauté sausage in Dutch oven until brown.
- Stir in tomato and green chiles, broth and seasoning and bring to boil.
- Stir in rice, cover and reduce heat.
- Simmer 25 minutes, uncover and cook until liquid absorbs.

Classic Macaroni and Tomato

2 cups elbow macaroni
1 (14 ounce) can stewed tomatoes with liquid
1 (8 ounce) package shredded cheddar cheese
2 tablespoons sugar
1 (6 ounce) package cheese slices

- Cook macaroni according to package directions and drain.
- In large mixing bowl, combine macaroni, tomatoes, shredded cheese, sugar, ¼ cup water and a little salt and mix well.
- Pour into 9 x 13-inch baking dish and place cheese slices on top.
- Bake at 350° for 30 minutes or until bubbly.

Traditional Hoppin' John

2 (16 ounce) cans jalapeno black-eyed peas with juice
¾ pound ham, chopped
1 cup chopped onion
2 cups hot cooked rice
½ cup chopped green onions

- In saucepan, combine peas, ham and onion.
- Bring to a boil, reduce heat and simmer 15 minutes.
- Stir in rice and green onions and serve hot.

Spinach Rice

1 cup uncooked instant rice
1 (10 ounce) package frozen chopped spinach
1 onion, finely chopped
3 tablespoons butter
¾ cup grated cheddar cheese

- Cook rice in large saucepan.

- Punch holes in box of spinach and cook in microwave about 3 minutes.

- Reserve 3 tablespoons cheese for topping and add spinach, onion, butter, cheese and ¼ teaspoon salt to rice. (If rice mixture seems a little dry, add several tablespoons water.)

- Pour into greased 2-quart baking dish and bake at 350° for 25 minutes.

Easy Fast Vegetables

Roasted Vegetable Medley

1½ pounds assorted fresh vegetables
1 (11 ounce) can water chestnuts, drained
1 (1 ounce) dry savory herb with garlic soup mix
2 tablespoons (¼ stick) butter, melted

- Cut all vegetables in uniform 2-inch pieces and place in greased 2-quart casserole dish with water chestnuts.
- Combine melted butter and soup mix, drizzle mixture over vegetables and stir well.
- Cover, bake vegetables at 400° for 20 to 25 minutes or until tender and stir once.

Use your favorite vegetables such as squash, carrots, red bell peppers, zucchini, cauliflower or broccoli.

Buttery Veggies

½ cup (1 stick) butter
2 yellow squash, sliced
1 (16 ounce) package broccoli florets
1 (10 ounce) box frozen corn

- Melt butter in large skillet and combine all vegetables.
- Sauté vegetables for 10 to 15 minutes or until tender-crisp.
- Add a little salt if you like and serve warm.

Shoe-Peg Corn Chile Casserole

½ cup (1 stick) butter
1 (8 ounce) package cream cheese
3 (16 ounce) cans shoe-peg corn, drained
1 (4 ounce) can chopped green chiles
1½ cups cracker crumbs

- Melt butter in saucepan, stir in cream cheese and mix until cream cheese melts.
- Add corn and chiles (and some salt and pepper if you like), mix and pour into greased baking dish.
- Sprinkle cracker crumbs over casserole and bake at 350° for 25 minutes.

Corn Olé

2 (10 ounce) packages frozen whole kernel corn
2 tablespoons (¼ stick) butter
1 (8 ounce) package cream cheese
1 tablespoon sugar
1 (4 ounce) can chopped green chiles

- Cook corn according to package directions, drain and set aside.
- Melt butter in saucepan over low heat, add cream cheese and stir until it melts.
- Stir in corn, sugar and green chiles and spoon into greased 2-quart baking dish.
- Cover and bake at 350° for 25 minutes.

Mexican Corn

2 (16 ounce) cans whole corn, drained
1 (8 ounce) package cream cheese
1 (4 ounce) can chopped green chiles
1 (2 ounce) jar pimentos

- Combine all ingredients in saucepan and mix well.
- Simmer over low heat until cheese melts.

Fabulous Fried Corn

2 (16 ounce) packages frozen whole kernel corn
½ cup (1 stick) butter
1 cup whipping cream
1 tablespoon sugar
1 teaspoon salt

- Place corn in large skillet over medium heat and add butter, whipping cream, sugar and salt.
- Stirring constantly, heat until most of whipping cream and butter absorbs into corn.

Yes, I know this has too many calories, but it's my grandkids' favorite vegetable. And who can turn down grandkids?

Venetian Corn

1 (16 ounce) package frozen whole kernel corn

2 slices bacon, cooked, diced

1 onion, chopped

1 (16 ounce) can Italian-style stewed tomatoes with liquid

- Combine all ingredients in 2-quart pan and cook until most of tomato liquid is gone.
- Add a little salt and pepper and serve hot.

Jambalaya in Minutes

¼ pound bacon

1 pound fresh okra, sliced

2 onions, chopped

1 (16 ounce) can stewed tomatoes with liquid

1 (16 ounce) can whole kernel corn, drained

- Fry bacon in large skillet until crisp and drain.
- In skillet with bacon drippings, sauté okra and onions but do not brown.
- Add tomatoes and corn and bring to a boil.
- Simmer about 5 to 10 minutes. (Jambalaya must not be runny.)
- Serve over hot rice and sprinkle bacon on top of each serving.

Lucky Black-Eyed Peas

2 (10 ounce) packages frozen black-eyed peas
1¼ cups chopped green pepper
¾ cup chopped onion 3 tablespoons butter
1 (15 ounce) can stewed tomatoes with liquid

- Cook black-eyed peas according to package directions and drain.
- Sauté green pepper and onion in butter.
- Add peas, tomatoes and a little salt and pepper.
- Cook over low heat until thoroughly heated and stir often.

Better Butter Beans

1 cup sliced celery
1 onion, chopped
¼ cup (½ stick) butter
1 (10 ounce) can diced tomatoes and green chiles
2 (15 ounce) cans butter beans

- Sauté celery and onion in butter for about 3 minutes
- Add tomatoes and chiles, several sprinkles of salt and about ½ teaspoon sugar.
- Add butter beans, cover and simmer about 20 minutes.
- Serve hot.

Creamy Green Peas

1 (16 ounce) package frozen English peas
2 tablespoons (¼ stick) butter
1 (10 ounce) can cream of celery soup
1 (3 ounce) package cream cheese
1 (8 ounce) can water chestnuts, drained

- Cook peas in microwave for 8 minutes and turn dish after 4 minutes.
- In large saucepan, combine butter, soup and cream cheese, cook on medium heat and stir until butter and cream cheese melt.
- Add peas and water chestnuts and mix.
- Serve hot.

Garlic Cheese Peas

1 (10 ounce) can cream of mushroom soup
1 (6 ounce) roll garlic cheese
2 (15 ounce) cans green peas, drained
⅛ teaspoon red pepper

- In saucepan, heat soup and cheese until cheese melts.
- Add peas and red pepper and heat thoroughly.

Creamy Swiss Peas

3 (15 ounce) cans green peas and onions, drained
1 (8 ounce) carton sour cream
1 (8 ounce) package grated Swiss cheese
2 cups crushed corn flakes

- In large bowl, combine peas and onions, sour cream, cheese and salt to taste.
- Spoon into buttered 3-quart baking dish and sprinkle corn flakes over top.
- Bake uncovered at 350° for 35 minutes.

Creamy Pimento Cabbage

1 medium head cabbage, cooked tender-crisp, drained
2 tablespoons (¼ stick) butter
1 tablespoon sugar
¼ teaspoon nutmeg
1 (4 ounce) jar pimentos, drained
1 (8 ounce) package cream cheese

- Combine cabbage, butter, sugar, nutmeg and pimentos in saucepan.
- Add cream cheese while on low heat and stir until cream cheese melts.

Carrots for the Kids

2 (15 ounce) cans carrots
¼ cup (½ stick) butter
3 tablespoons brown sugar
1 teaspoon brown ginger

- Drain carrots but reserve 2 tablespoons liquid.
- Combine reserved liquid with butter, brown sugar and ginger and heat thoroughly.
- Add carrots, stir gently and cook for 3 minutes.
- Serve hot.

Nutty Green Beans

1 (16 ounce) package frozen green beans
¼ cup (½ stick) butter
¾ cup pine nuts
¼ teaspoon garlic powder
Salt and pepper

- Cook beans in water in covered 3-quart saucepan for 10 to 15 minutes or until tender-crisp and drain.
- Melt butter in skillet over medium heat, add pine nuts and cook, stirring frequently, until golden.
- Add pine nuts to green beans and add seasonings.
- Serve hot.

Broccoli Parmesan

1 (16 ounce) package frozen broccoli spears
½ teaspoon garlic powder
½ cup breadcrumbs
¼ cup (½ stick) butter, melted
½ cup parmesan cheese

- Cook broccoli as directed on package and drain.
- Add garlic powder, breadcrumbs, butter and cheese (and some salt if you like) and toss.
- Heat and serve.

Broccoli Lemón

2 (16 ounce) packages of broccoli florets
¼ cup (½ stick) butter
1 tablespoon lemon juice
½ teaspoon seasoned salt

- Cook broccoli according to package directions and drain.
- Melt butter and stir in lemon juice and seasoned salt.
- Pour butter mixture over broccoli and toss to coat.

Broccoli-Stuffed Tomatoes

4 medium tomatoes
1 (10 ounce) package frozen chopped broccoli
1 (6 ounce) roll garlic cheese, softened
$\frac{1}{2}$ teaspoon garlic salt

- Cut tops off tomatoes and scoop out pulp.
- Cook broccoli according to package directions and drain well.
- Combine broccoli, cheese and garlic salt and heat just until cheese melts.
- Stuff broccoli mixture into tomatoes and place on baking sheet.
- Bake at 375° for about 10 minutes.

Crumbly Tomatoes

2 (16 ounce) cans diced tomatoes, drained
$1\frac{1}{2}$ cups toasted breadcrumbs, divided
Scant $\frac{1}{4}$ cup sugar
$\frac{1}{2}$ onion, chopped
$\frac{1}{4}$ cup ($\frac{1}{2}$ stick) butter, melted

- Combine tomatoes, 1 cup breadcrumbs, sugar, onion and butter.
- Pour into buttered baking dish and cover with remaining breadcrumbs.
- Bake at 325° for 25 to 30 minutes or until crumbs are light brown.

Parmesan Eggplant Bake

1 eggplant
½ cup mayonnaise
⅔ cup seasoned breadcrumbs
¼ cup grated parmesan cheese

- Peel eggplant and slice ½-inch thick.
- Spread both sides of eggplant slices with mayonnaise and dip in mixture of crumbs and cheese until coated well.
- Place in single layer in shallow baking dish and bake at 400° for 20 minutes.

Eggplant Fries

1 medium eggplant
1 egg, beaten
3 tablespoons flour
½ teaspoon salt
½ teaspoon baking powder

- Peel and slice eggplant, steam until tender and drain.
- Mash eggplant until smooth.
- Add egg, flour, salt and baking powder and mix well.
- Form into patties and deep fry in hot oil.

Jack Squash

5 cups squash, cooked, drained
¾ cup grated Monterey Jack cheese
1 (10 ounce) can cream of chicken soup
1 (16 ounce) box herb dressing mix

- Place cooked squash in mixing bowl and season with salt to taste.
- Add cheese and soup and blend well.
- Mix dressing according to package directions and place half dressing in greased 9 x 13-inch baking dish.
- Spoon in squash mixture and sprinkle remaining dressing on top.
- Bake uncovered at 375° for 30 minutes.

Chile-Squash Casserole

6 medium yellow squash, sliced
1 yellow onion, chopped
1 (8 ounce) jar processed cheese spread
1 (4 ounce) can chopped green chiles

- Boil squash and onion until tender and drain well.
- Mix with cheese and chiles.
- Pour into buttered 7 x 11-inch baking dish and bake at 375° for 15 minutes.

Sweet 'n Creamy Squash

6 to 8 medium yellow squash

1 (8 ounce) package cream cheese, softened, cubed

2 tablespoons ($\frac{1}{4}$ stick) butter

1 teaspoon sugar

- Cut up squash, place in saucepan with a little water, boil until tender and drain.

- Add cream cheese, butter, sugar and a little salt and pepper.

- Cook over low heat and stir until cream cheese melts.

Creamy Spinach Bake

2 (10 ounce) packages frozen chopped spinach

2 (3 ounce) packages cream cheese, softened

3 tablespoons butter

1 cup seasoned breadcrumbs

- Cook spinach according to package directions and drain.

- Combine cream cheese and butter with spinach and heat until they melt and mix well with spinach.

- Pour into greased baking dish and sprinkle a little salt over spinach.

- Cover with breadcrumbs and bake at 350° for 15 to 20 minutes.

French Onion Spinach

2 (10 ounce) packages frozen chopped spinach, thawed,
    well drained
1 (1 ounce) package dry onion soup mix
1 (8 ounce) carton sour cream
⅔ cup shredded Monterey Jack cheese

- Combine spinach, onion soup mix and sour cream and pour into buttered 2-quart baking dish.
- Bake at 350° for 20 minutes.
- Remove from oven, sprinkle cheese over top and return casserole to oven for 5 more minutes.

Souper Cauliflower

1 (16 ounce) package frozen cauliflower, cooked, drained
1 (10 ounce) can cream of celery soup
¼ cup milk
1 cup shredded cheddar cheese

- Place cauliflower in greased 2-quart baking dish.
- In saucepan, combine soup, milk and cheese and heat just enough to mix well.
- Pour mixture over cauliflower and bake at 350° for 15 minutes.

Creamy Sesame Cauliflower

1 (16 ounce) package frozen cauliflower
Salt and pepper
1 (8 ounce) carton sour cream
1½ cups grated American or cheddar cheese
4 teaspoons sesame seeds, toasted

- Cook cauliflower according to package directions, drain and place half cauliflower in 2-quart baking dish.
- Sprinkle a little salt and pepper on cauliflower and spread with half sour cream and half cheese.
- Top with 2 teaspoons sesame seeds and repeat layers.
- Bake at 350° for about 15 to 20 minutes.

Asparagus-Ham Roll-Ups

4 slices Swiss cheese
2 (10 ounce) cans asparagus spears
4 slices ham
1 (10 ounce) can cream of celery soup

- Place 1 slice cheese and 3 asparagus spears on each ham slice. Roll up and secure with toothpick.
- Place each roll-up in casserole dish, seam side down.
- In saucepan, dilute soup with ⅓ cup water and heat just enough to mix well.
- Pour over roll-ups and bake at 350° for 15 to 20 minutes.

Aspire to Be Asparagus

6 fresh asparagus spears, trimmed
1 tablespoon butter
1 teaspoon lemon juice
1 teaspoon sesame seeds

- Place asparagus in skillet (sprinkle with salt if desired), add ¼ cup water and bring to a boil.
- Reduce heat, cover and simmer for 4 minutes.
- Melt butter and add lemon juice and sesame seeds.
- Drain asparagus and drizzle with butter mixture.

Creamy Vegetable Casserole

1 (16 ounce) package frozen broccoli, carrots and cauliflower
1 (10 ounce) can cream of mushroom soup
1 (8 ounce) carton garden vegetable cream cheese
1 cup seasoned croutons

- Cook vegetables according to package directions, drain and place in large bowl.
- Place soup and cream cheese in saucepan and heat just enough to mix easily.
- Pour soup mixture into vegetable mixture, stir well and pour into 2-quart baking dish.
- Sprinkle with croutons and bake uncovered at 375° for 25 minutes or until bubbly.

• •

Creamy Vegetable Medley

**1 (16 ounce) package frozen broccoli, cauliflower and
carrots**
1 (16 ounce) package frozen corn
2 (10 ounce) cans nacho cheese soup
½ cup milk

- Combine vegetable mixture and corn in greased 2-quart
  baking dish.
- Combine nacho cheese soup and milk in saucepan and
  heat just enough to mix well.
- Pour soup mixture over vegetables, cover and bake at
  350° for 30 minutes.

Mexi-Corn

3 (15 ounce) cans whole kernel corn, drained
1 (10 ounce) can tomatoes and green chiles, drained
1 (8 ounce) package shredded Monterey Jack cheese
1 cup cheese cracker crumbs

- In large bowl, combine corn, tomatoes and green chiles
  and cheese and mix well.
- Pour into buttered 2½-quart baking dish.
- Sprinkle cracker crumbs over casserole.
- Bake uncovered at 350° for 25 minutes.

Mushrooms and Corn

4 ounces fresh mushrooms, sliced
3 fresh green onions with tops, chopped
¼ cup (½ stick) butter
1 (15 ounce) package frozen whole kernel corn

- Place all ingredients in 2-quart saucepan and cook over medium heat for 5 to 10 minutes.
- Add salt and pepper to taste.

Herb-Seasoned Vegetables

1 (14 ounce) can seasoned chicken broth with Italian herbs
½ teaspoon garlic powder
1 (16 ounce) package frozen vegetables
½ cup grated parmesan cheese

- Heat broth, garlic powder and vegetables to a boil.
- Cover and cook over low heat for 5 minutes or until tender-crisp and drain.
- Place vegetables in serving dish and sprinkle with cheese.

Easy Fast
Chicken
and
Turkey
Main Dishes

Peach Salsa Chicken

1 pound boneless, skinless chicken breast halves

3 tablespoons taco seasoning

1 (11 ounce) jar chunky salsa

1 cup peach preserves

- Cut chicken into ½-inch cubes.
- Place chicken in large, resealable plastic bag, add taco seasoning and toss to coat.
- In skillet, brown chicken in a little oil.
- Combine salsa and preserves, stir into skillet and bring mixture to a boil.
- Reduce heat, cover and simmer until juices run clear. Serve over rice or noodles.

Green Chile Chicken

5 boneless, skinless chicken breast halves

1 (1 ounce) package hot and spicy recipe coating mixture

1 (4 ounce) can chopped green chiles

Chunky salsa

- Dredge chicken in coating mixture and place in greased 9 x 13-inch baking dish.
- Bake at 375° for 25 minutes.
- Remove from oven, spread green chiles over chicken breasts and return to oven for 5 minutes.
- Serve with salsa over each chicken breast.

Chicken and Rice Voila!

3 boneless, chicken breasts halves, cut into strips
1 (14 ounce) can chicken broth seasoned with Italian herbs
¾ cup uncooked rice
¼ cup grated parmesan cheese

- Cook chicken in non-stick skillet until brown, stirring often, and remove.
- Add broth and rice to skillet and heat to a boil.
- Cover and simmer over low heat for 25 minutes. (Add more water if necessary.)
- Stir in cheese and return chicken to pan.
- Cover and cook for 5 minutes or until done.

Pineapple Chicken with Rice

4 boneless, skinless chicken breast halves, cubed
1 (20 ounce) can pineapple chunks with juice
½ cup honey mustard grill-and-glaze sauce
1 red bell pepper, chopped

- In skillet with a little oil, brown chicken and cook on low heat for 15 minutes.
- Add pineapple, honey mustard and bell pepper and bring to a boil.
- Reduce heat to low and simmer for 10 to 15 minutes or until sauce thickens slightly.
- Serve over hot cooked rice.

Ranch Chicken Dijon

¼ cup prepared ranch salad dressing

1 tablespoon dijon-style mustard

4 boneless, skinless chicken breast halves

2 tablespoons (¼ stick) butter

3 tablespoons white wine or chicken broth

- In bowl, combine salad dressing and mustard and set aside.

- In skillet, cook chicken in butter and let simmer for 10 to 15 minutes.

- Add wine or broth and simmer another 20 minutes.

- Whisk in mustard mixture, cook and stir until blended and heated through.

- Serve over instant long grain and wild rice.

Fast Chicken

4 boneless, skinless chicken breast halves

20 saltine crackers, crushed

2 eggs, beaten

¼ teaspoon black pepper

- Pound chicken breasts to ¼-inch thickness.

- Combine eggs, pepper and 2 tablespoons water.

- Dip chicken in egg mixture and crushed crackers and coat well.

- Deep fry until golden brown and drain well.

Chicken Spaghetti

1 (10 ounce) package thin spaghetti

1 (10 ounce) package frozen sugar snap peas

2 tablespoons butter

3 cups rotisserie cooked chicken strips

1 (11 ounce) can mandarin oranges, drained

⅔ cup stir-fry sauce

- Cook spaghetti according to package directions; stir in sugar snap peas and cook an additional minute. Drain and stir in butter until butter melts. Spoon into bowl.

- Add chicken strips, oranges and stir-fry sauce; toss to coat.

Juicy Baked Chicken

¼ pound (1stick) butter, melted

2 tablespoons mayonnaise

2 tablespoons white wine Worcestershire sauce

1 (6 ounce) can french-fried onions, crushed

6 boneless, skinless chicken breasts halves

- Preheat oven to 375°. In shallow bowl, combine melted butter, mayonnaise and Worcestershire sauce. Place crushed onions in another shallow bowl.

- Dry chicken breasts with paper towels and dip first into butter mixture and dredge each chicken breast in crushed onions. Place in large baking pan, arranging so pieces do not touch.

- Bake 25 minutes or until chicken juices run clear.

Quiet Drumsticks

1 (20 ounce) package frozen chicken drum sticks

Sauce:

½ cup hoisin sauce

2 tablespoons light soy sauce

1 teaspoon minced garlic

- Preheat broiler. Place drumsticks in a single layer, in greased 9 x 13-inch baking dish and broil for 10 minutes. Turn drumsticks and broil another 10 minutes. Reduce heat to 325°.

- In bowl, combine hoisin sauce, soy sauce and garlic, mixing well. Brush chicken drumsticks lightly with sauce and bake for 25 minutes. During baking time, remove from oven and brush with remaining sauce and continue cooking until glaze bubbles and browns.

Honey-Roasted Chicken

3 tablespoons soy sauce

3 tablespoon honey

2 ½ cups crushed wheat cereal

½ cup very finely minced walnuts

5–6 boneless, skinless chicken breast halves

- Preheat oven to 400°. In shallow bowl, combine soy sauce and honey and set aside. In another shallow bowl, combine crushed cereal and walnuts.

- Dip both sides of each chicken breast in soy sauce-honey mixture and dredge in cereal-walnut mixture. Place each piece on sprayed foil-lined baking sheet. Bake for 25 minutes (about 35 minutes if breasts are very large).

Creamy Chicken with Veggies

6 small boneless, skinless chicken breast halves
Seasoned pepper
Oil
1 (16 ounce) bottle creamy Italian dressing
1 (16 ounce) package frozen broccoli, cauliflower and
carrots, thawed

- Sprinkle chicken with seasoned pepper and salt to taste.
  Place a little oil in large, heavy non-stick skillet over
  medium-high heat. Add chicken breasts and cook 4
  minutes on each side. Pour about three-fourths dressing
  over chicken; cover and simmer for about 8 minutes.

- Add vegetables, cover and cook another 10 minutes or
  until vegetables are tender.

Chicken Cashew Stir-Fry

1 pound chicken tenders, cut into strips
1 (16 ounce) package frozen broccoli, cauliflower and
carrots
1 (8 ounce) jar stir-fry sauce
⅓ cup cashew halves
1 (12 ounce) package chow mein noodles

- In 12-inch wok, place a little oil and stir-fry chicken
  strips over high heat about 4 minutes. Add vegetables
  and stir-fry another 4 minutes or until vegetables are
  tender.

- Stir in stir-fry sauce and cashews. Cook just until
  mixture is hot. Serve over chow mein noodles.

Summer's Coming Chicken

6 large boneless, skinless chicken breast halves

1 (6 ounce) can frozen limeade concentrate, thawed

3 tablespoons brown sugar

½ cup chili sauce

Hot, buttered rice

- Sprinkle chicken breasts with a little salt and pepper and place in lightly greased skillet. Cook on high heat and brown on both sides for about 10 minutes. Remove from skillet, but set aside and keep warm.

- Add limeade concentrate, brown sugar and chili sauce to skillet. Bring to boil and cook, stirring constantly, for 10 minutes.

- Return chicken to skillet and spoon sauce over chicken. Reduce heat, cover and simmer for 15 minutes. Serve over hot, buttered rice.

Honey-Mustard Chicken

⅓ cup dijon-style mustard

½ cup honey

2 tablespoons dried dill

1 (2½ pound) chicken, quartered

- Combine mustard, honey and dill.

- Arrange chicken quarters in 9 x 13-inch baking dish.

- Pour mustard mixture over chicken. Turn chicken over and make sure mustard mixture covers chicken.

- Bake covered at 375° for 30 minutes. Uncover and bake another 10 minutes.

Chicken Tortellini Supper

1 (9 ounce) package refrigerated cheese tortellini
1 (10 ounce) package frozen green peas, thawed
1 (8 ounce) carton cream cheese with chives and onion
½ teaspoon Tony Chachere's spicing seasoning
½ cup sour cream
1 (9 ounce) package frozen cooked chicken breasts

- Cook cheese tortellini in saucepan according to package directions. Place peas in colander and pour hot pasta water over green peas. Return tortellini and peas to saucepan.

- Combine cream cheese, spicy seasoning and sour cream in smaller saucepan and heat on low, stirring well until cream cheese melts. Spoon mixture over tortellini and peas and toss, keeping heat on low.

- Heat cooked chicken in microwave according to package directions. Spoon tortellini and peas in serving bowl and place chicken on top. Serve hot.

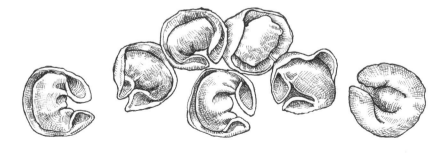

Pimento Cheese Chicken

4 large skinless, boneless chicken breast halves

½ cup milk

1 large egg, beaten

2 cups seasoned breadcrumbs

1 (16 ounce) carton prepared pimento cheese

- Preheat oven to 350°. Dry chicken breasts with paper towels and sprinkle well with salt and pepper.

- Combine milk and beaten egg in shallow bowl, mixing well and place breadcrumbs in second shallow bowl. Dip chicken in milk mixture and dredge in breadcrumbs.

- In large skillet over medium-high heat, pour in a little oil to ⅛-inch depth and cook chicken about 10 to 12 minutes on each side. Transfer to baking sheet. Hold chicken with tongs and cut slit in 1 side of each chicken breast to form a pocket. Spoon about ¼ cup pimento cheese into each pocket and bake another 5 minutes or until cheese melts.

Stir-Fry Chicken with Noodles

1 pound boneless, skinless chicken breast halves
1½ cups sliced mushrooms
1½ cups bell pepper strips
1 cup sweet-and-sour stir-fry sauce
1 (16 ounce) package spaghetti, cooked, drained
¼ cup (½ stick) butter

- Salt and pepper chicken and cut into thin slices. In large skillet with a little oil, brown chicken slices and cook for 5 minutes on low-medium heat. Transfer to plate and reserve.

- In same skillet adding a little more oil, stir-fry mushrooms and bell pepper strips for 5 minutes. Add chicken strips and sweet-and-sour sauce, stirring until ingredients are thoroughly hot.

- While spaghetti is still hot and drained, add butter, stirring until butter is melted. Place in large bowl and toss with chicken mixture. Serve hot.

Honey Turkey Tenders

Oil

1 pound turkey tenders

1 (6 ounce) package roasted-garlic long grain, wild rice

Glaze:

⅔ cup honey

2 teaspoons grated, peeled fresh ginger

1 tablespoon white wine Worcestershire sauce

1 tablespoon soy sauce

1 tablespoon lemon juice

- Place a little oil in heavy skillet and cook turkey tenders about 5 minutes on each side or until brown.

- Combine all glaze ingredients, mix well and pour into skillet. Bring mixture to a boil, reduce heat and simmer for 15 minutes; spoon glaze over turkey every 5 minutes.

- Prepare rice according to package directions and serve turkey over hot rice.

Fast Chicken Dinner

1 (16 ounce) package frozen broccoli florets, thawed

1 (10 ounce) can cream of chicken soup

⅔ cup mayonnaise

1 cup shredded cheddar cheese

3 cups cooked, cubed chicken

2 cups crushed cheese crackers

- Preheat oven to 375°. In large bowl, combine broccoli, soup, mayonnaise, cheese and chicken, mixing well. Pour into greased 3-quart baking dish; cover and bake 20 minutes.

- Uncover and sprinkle cheese crackers over top of casserole and return to oven for another 10 minutes.

Creamy Chicken Pasta

1 (10 ounce) package penne pasta

1 tablespoon olive oil

2 (12 ounce) cans white chicken meat, drained

2 tablespoons prepared pesto

¾ cup whipping cream

- In large saucepan, cook penne pasta according to package directions. Drain and place back in saucepan. Gently stir in oil, chicken, prepared pesto (for a stronger basil or garlic taste, you might want to use a little more than the 2 tablespoon pesto), whipping cream and salt and pepper to taste.

- Place saucepan over low heat and simmer, stirring often, (but do not let mixture boil) until cream is absorbed into pasta. Spoon into serving bowl and serve immediately.

Grilled Chicken Cordon Bleu

6 boneless, skinless chicken breast halves

6 slices Swiss cheese, divided

6 thin slices deli ham

3 tablespoons oil

1 cup seasoned breadcrumbs

- Flatten chicken to ¼-inch thickness and place 1 slice each of cheese and ham on each piece of chicken to within ¼ inch of edges.
- Fold in half and secure with toothpicks.
- Brush chicken with oil and roll in breadcrumbs.
- Grill, covered, over medium-high heat for 15 to 18 minutes or until juices run clear.

Chicken Quesadillas

6 boneless, skinless chicken breast halves, cubed

1 (10 ounce) can cheddar cheese soup

⅔ cup chunky salsa 10 flour tortillas

- Cook chicken in skillet until juices evaporate and stir often.
- Add soup and salsa and heat thoroughly.
- Spread about ⅓ cup soup mixture on half tortilla to within ½-inch of edge.
- Moisten edges of tortillas with water, fold over and seal.
- Place tortillas on 2 baking sheets (5 tortillas each) and bake at 400° for 5 to 6 minutes.

T-Ball's Tonight Enchiladas

2½ to 3 cups cooked, cubed chicken breast

1 (10 ounce) can cream of chicken soup

1½ cups chunky salsa, divided

8 (6 inch) flour tortillas

1 (10 ounce) can fiesta nacho cheese soup

- In saucepan, combine chicken, cream of chicken soup and ½ cup salsa and heat.

- Spoon about ⅓ cup chicken mixture down center of each tortilla and roll tortilla around filling.

- Place rolled tortillas seam-side down in sprayed 9 x 13-inch baking dish.

- Mix nacho cheese soup, remaining salsa and ¼ cup water and pour over enchiladas.

- Cover with wax paper and microwave on HIGH, turning several times, for 5 minutes or until bubbly.

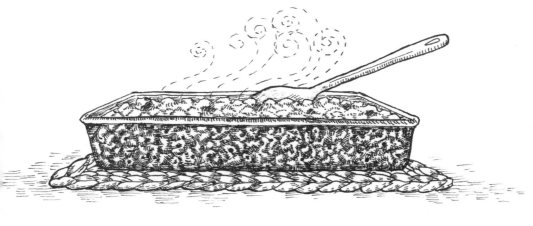

Fast Cranberry Stuffing

1 (14 ounce) can chicken broth
1 rib celery, chopped
½ cup fresh or frozen cranberries
1 small onion, chopped
4 cups herb-seasoned stuffing

- Mix broth, celery, cranberries, onion and a dash of black pepper in saucepan and heat to boil.
- Cover and cook over low heat for 5 minutes.
- Add stuffing, mix lightly and spoon into baking dish.
- Bake at 325° just until thoroughly heated.

Plum-Good Turkey

2 cups red plum jam
1 cup maple syrup
1 teaspoon dry mustard
¼ cup lemon juice
1 (5 pound) bone-in turkey breast

- In saucepan, combine plum jam, syrup, mustard and lemon juice and bring to a boil.
- Turn down heat and simmer for about 20 minutes or until thick. Reserve 1 cup.
- Place turkey breast in roasting pan, pour remaining glaze over turkey and bake according to directions on turkey breast package.
- Slice turkey and serve with heated reserved glaze.

Easy Fast
Beef
Main Dishes

Oriental Beef and Noodles

1¼ pounds ground beef

2 (3 ounce) packages oriental-flavored ramen noodles

1 (16 ounce) package frozen oriental stir-fry vegetable mixture

½ teaspoon ground ginger

3 tablespoons thinly sliced green onions

- In large skillet, brown ground beef and drain.
- Add ½ cup water, salt and pepper, simmer 10 minutes, and transfer to separate bowl.
- In same skillet, combine 2 cups water, vegetables, noodles (broken up), ginger and both seasoning packets.
- Bring to a boil and reduce heat.
- Cover, simmer 3 minutes or until noodles are tender and stir occasionally.
- Return beef to skillet and stir in green onions. Serve right from skillet.

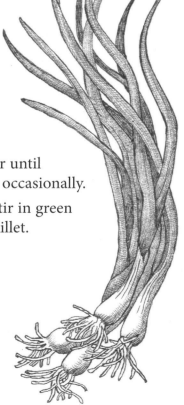

Onion Beef Steaks

1½ pounds lean ground beef
⅓ cup salsa
⅓ cup butter cracker crumbs
1 (10 ounce) can cream of onion soup

- Combine beef, salsa and cracker crumbs and form into 5 to 6 patties.
- Brown patties in skillet and reduce heat.
- Add ¼ cup water and simmer for 15 minutes.
- In saucepan, combine onion soup and ½ cup water or milk, heat and mix.
- Pour mixture over beef patties and serve over hot, cooked noodles.

Salsa Skillet

1 pound lean ground beef
1 (10 ounce) can tomato soup
1 cup chunky salsa or picante sauce
6 (6 inch) flour tortillas, cut into 1-inch pieces
1¼ cups shredded cheddar cheese, divided

- Brown beef in skillet and drain.
- Add soup, salsa, ¾ cup water, tortilla pieces, ½ teaspoon salt and half of cheese.
- Bring to a boil, cover and cook over low heat 5 minutes.
- Top with remaining cheese and serve right from skillet.

A good family dish!

Spicy Beef with Noodles

1 pound lean ground beef

1 (1 ounce) package taco seasoning mix

1 (16 ounce) can Mexican-style stewed tomatoes with
   liquid

1 (16 ounce) can kidney beans with liquid

1 (1 pound) package egg noodles

- Cook beef in skillet and drain.
- Add taco seasoning and ½ cup water and simmer 15 minutes.
- Add stewed tomatoes and kidney beans. (You may need to add ¼ teaspoon salt.)
- Cook egg noodles according to package directions and serve beef over noodles.

Stadium Pie

2 (20 ounce) cans chili without beans

1 (16 ounce) package small corn chips

1 onion, chopped

1 (16 ounce) package shredded cheddar cheese

- Heat chili in saucepan.
- In 9 x 13-inch baking dish, layer corn chips, chili, onion and cheese one-third at a time. Repeat layers with cheese on top.
- Bake at 325° for 20 minutes or until cheese bubbles.

Steak with Creamy Horseradish Sauce

1 (2 pound) 1-inch thick sirloin steak

1 (8 ounce) carton sour cream

4 tablespoons prepared, bottled horseradish

- Preheat broiler. Pat steak dry and sprinkle liberally with salt and pepper. Broil steak on rack about 3 inches from heat for about 5 minutes. Let stand 5 minutes before slicing.

- In bowl, combine sour cream, horseradish, and a little salt and pepper, mixing well. Serve with sirloin steak.

Zingy Meat Loaf Sauce

1 (8 ounce) can tomato sauce

3 tablespoons brown sugar

1 tablespoon vinegar

1 tablespoon Worcestershire sauce

- In saucepan, combine all ingredients and heat, stirring constantly until mixture is thoroughly hot.

- Mixture may be spooned over meatloaf last 10 minutes of cooking time or spooned over each serving. This sauce is also tasty served over beef patties.

Yum, Yum Hot Dogs

10 (8-inch) flour tortillas
10 beef hot dogs
1 (15 ounce) can chili with beans, slightly heated
1 (16 ounce) can thick-and-chunky salsa
1 (8 ounce) package Mexican-style shredded cheese

- Preheat oven to 325°. Grease a 9 x 13-inch baking dish. Soften tortillas as directed on package.

- Place 1 hot dog and about 3 tablespoons chili on each tortilla and roll tortillas. Place seam-side down on baking dish. Pour salsa over tortillas.

- Cover with foil and bake 25 minutes. Remove from oven, uncover and sprinkle cheese over tortillas. Return to oven for 5 minutes.

Mexican Pizza

1 (12-inch) purchased pizza crust
1 (12 ounce) package Mexican style shredded cheese, divided
1 pound cooked and shredded barbecue
1 (4 ounce) sliced ripe olives, drained

- Preheat oven to 400°. Place pizza crust on baking sheet and sprinkle on half of cheese. Spread the shredded barbecue beef over top of cheese and sprinkle remaining cheese over top. Arrange olives over top of pizza.

- Bake 15 to 10 minutes or until hot and bubbly.

Stove-Top Nachos

½ (16 ounce) package tortilla chips
1 (8 ounce) can whole kernel corn, drained
1 cup chili beans (from 15 ounce can)
½ cup thick-and-chunky salsa, extra salsa for garnish
1 (8 ounce) package shredded 4-cheese blend
1 (4 ounce) can ripe olives, sliced

- Arrange tortilla chips in single layer in large 12-inch skillet (use a skillet that you can take to the table). In saucepan, combine corn, beans and salsa and heat just until hot and bubbly.

- Spoon salsa mixture over tortilla chips, then sprinkle on about three-fourths cheese. Cover skillet and cook on medium high heat about 5 minutes or until cheese melts.

- To serve, sprinkle ripe olives and remaining cheese over top. You may want to serve with more salsa.

Tomato Garlic Steak

2 (15 ounce) cans tomato soup with roasted garlic and herbs
½ cup Italian salad dressing
⅓ cup water
1½ pounds (¾-inch) boneless beef sirloin steak

- In saucepan, combine soups, dressing and water.
- Broil steaks to desired doneness. (Allow 15 minutes for medium.)
- Turn once and brush often with sauce.
- Heat remaining sauce to serve with steak.

Steak and Rice

1 pound round steak, cut in strips
1 (14 ounce) can beef broth
3 tablespoons cornstarch
1 tablespoon soy sauce
1 red bell pepper, julienned
1 green bell pepper, julienned

- In large skillet brown steak strips; reduce heat, add ⅓ cup water, cover and simmer until liquid evaporates.

- Combine beef broth, cornstarch and soy sauce (and a little garlic powder if you like) and pour over steak strips. Add bell peppers, stirring until mixture boils and thickens. Serve over hot cooked rice.

Skillet Steak

2 teaspoons oil
2 teaspoons minced garlic
½ teaspoon cayenne pepper
2 tablespoons soy sauce
2 tablespoons honey
1 pound beef sirloin, thinly sliced

- Combine oil, garlic, cayenne pepper, soy sauce and honey and place in plastic freezer bag. Add sliced beef, seal and shake; refrigerate for 25 minutes.

- Place beef mixture in large greased skillet over medium-high heat and cook 5 to 6 minutes or until desired doneness, but do not over-cook. Serve over hot cooked rice.

Beef with Mushroom Gravy

1 pound lean ground beef
¼ cup chili sauce
1 egg
¾ cup crushed corn flakes
2 (10 ounce) cans cream of mushroom soup

- In bowl, combine ground beef, chili sauce, egg, crushed corn flakes and salt and pepper to taste, mixing well. Shape into 4 patties, about ¾-inch thick.

- Place patties in skillet with a tiny bit of oil and on high heat, brown each patty on both sides. Reduce heat, cover and simmer for 10 to 15 minutes.

- Stir in both cans soup with ½ cup water, mixing well. Spoon gravy over patties and let simmer for about 10 minutes. This gravy is great served over mashed potatoes or hot biscuits.

Winter Chili

1 (40 ounce) can chili with beans
1 (7 ounce) can chopped green chilies
1 bunch fresh green onions, sliced
1 (8 ounce) package shredded Mexican 4-cheese blend
2½ cups crushed ranch-flavored tortilla chips, divided

- Preheat oven to 350°. Combine chili, green chilies, onions, cheese and 2 cups crushed chips. Transfer to greased 3-quart baking dish and bake 20 minutes.

- Remove from oven and sprinkle remaining chips over top of casserole and continue baking another 10 minutes.

Asian Grilled Steak

1½ pound flank-steak

¼ cup low-sodium soy sauce

Sauce:

¼ cup sugar

¼ cup ketchup

3 tablespoons cider vinegar

1 tablespoon bottled ground fresh ginger

¼ teaspoon cayenne pepper

- Place flank-steak in a large baggie and pour the ¼ cup (60 ml) soy sauce over steak. Seal but move steak around getting soy sauce over all of steak.

- In bowl, combine sugar, ketchup, vinegar, ginger and cayenne pepper. Place steak on hot grill and cook about 5 minutes on each side, basting several times during cooking. Cut steak diagonally across grain and drizzle with remaining sauce mixture.

Beef 'n Cheese Gnocchi

1 pound lean ground beef

1 (10 ounce) can cheddar cheese soup

1 (10 ounce) can tomato bisque soup

2 cups uncooked gnocchi or shell pasta

- In skillet, cook beef until brown and drain.

- Add soups, 1½ cups water and pasta and bring mixture to a boil.

- Cover and cook over medium heat for 10 to 12 minutes or until pasta is done. Stir often.

Texas Taco Pie

1 pound lean ground beef

1 large bell pepper, seeded, chopped

2 jalapeno peppers, seeded, chopped

1 (15 ounce) can Mexican stewed tomatoes

1 tablespoon chili powder

1 (8 ounce) box corn muffin mix

1 egg

⅓ cup milk

1 (8 ounce) package shredded sharp cheddar cheese

- Brown ground beef, bell pepper and jalapeno peppers in large skillet with a little oil; drain. Stir in tomatoes, chili powder, ½ cup water and a little salt to taste. Cover and cook on medium heat for about 10 minutes or until most liquid cooks out, but not dry.

- Pour into greased 9 x 13-inch baking pan and sprinkle with cheese. Combine muffin mix, egg and milk and pour over meat mixture.

- Bake 20 minutes or until corn muffin mix is light brown.

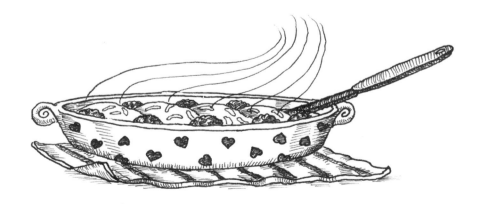

Pepper Steak

1 (1¼ pound) sirloin steak, cut in strips Seasoned salt

1 (16 ounce) package frozen bell pepper and onion strips, thawed

1 (16 ounce) package cubed Mexican processed cheese

- Sprinkle steak with seasoned salt.
- Coat large skillet with non-stick vegetable spray and cook steak strips for 10 minutes or until no longer pink.
- Remove steak from skillet and set aside.
- Stir in vegetables and ½ cup water and simmer vegetables for 5 minutes or until all liquid cooks out.
- Add processed cheese and turn heat to medium-low.
- When cheese melts, stir in steak and serve over hot cooked rice.

Easy Fast
Pork
Main Dishes

Ham with Orange-Raisin Sauce

1 (½-inch thick) slice fully cooked ham

1 cup orange juice

2 tablespoons brown sugar

1½ tablespoons cornstarch

⅓ cup white raisins

- Place ham slice in shallow baking dish.
- In saucepan, combine orange juice, brown sugar, cornstarch and raisins.
- Bring to boil, stirring constantly, until mixture thickens and pour over ham slice.
- Warm at 350° for about 20 minutes.

Excellent Orange-Raisin Sauce for Ham

⅔ cup orange juice

⅓ cup water

2 tablespoons brown sugar

1½ tablespoons cornstarch

⅓ cup light raisins

- Mix all ingredients in saucepan.
- Heat and cook, stirring constantly, until sauce thickens and is clear and bubbly.
- Serve with pre-cooked ham.

Orange Ham with Apples

½ cup orange marmalade

2 teaspoons butter

¼ teaspoon ground ginger

2 (½-inch thick) ham slices (about 2½ pounds)

4 apples, quartered

- Combine marmalade, butter and ginger in 1-cup glass measuring cup.
- Microwave on HIGH for 1 minute or until mixture melts and stir once.
- Cook ham covered with apples. Cover with grill lid and cook over medium-hot coals.
- Turn occasionally and baste with marmalade mixture, about 20 minutes.

Juicy Pork Chops

4 (½-inch thick) pork chops

1 tablespoon oil

1 (10 ounce) can cream of onion soup

2 tablespoons soy sauce

- In skillet, brown pork chops in oil.
- Cook chops for 15 minutes, drain and set aside.
- In same skillet, combine soup and soy sauce and heat to a boil.
- Return chops to pan, reduce heat to low and cover.
- Simmer for 20 minutes.

Pork ala Salsa

1 pound pork tenderloin, cubed
2 tablespoons taco seasoning
1 cup chunky salsa
⅓ cup peach preserves

- Toss pork with taco seasoning and brown with a little oil in skillet.
- Stir in salsa and preserves and bring to a boil.
- Lower heat and simmer for 10 minutes.
- Pour over hot cooked rice to serve.

Mexican Casserole

1 pound pork sausage
2 (15 ounce) cans pork and beans
1 (15 ounce) can Mexican-style stewed tomatoes
1 (8 ounce) package cornbread muffin mix

- Brown sausage and drain fat.
- Add beans and tomatoes, blend and bring to a boil.
- Pour mixture into 3-quart greased casserole dish.
- Prepare muffin mix according to package directions and drop by teaspoonfuls over meat-bean mixture.
- Bake at 400° for 30 minutes or until top browns.

Sweet Praline Ham

2 (½-inch thick) ham slices, cooked (about 2½ pounds)
½ cup maple syrup
3 tablespoons brown sugar
1 tablespoon butter
⅓ cup chopped pecans

- Heat ham slices in shallow pan at 325° for 10 minutes.
- Bring syrup, sugar and butter to boil in small saucepan and stir often.
- Stir in pecans and spoon syrup mixture over ham.
- Warm another 20 minutes.

Easy Fast
Seafood
Main Dishes

Classic Baked Fish

1 pound fish filets
3 tablespoons butter
1 teaspoon tarragon
2 teaspoons capers
2 tablespoons lemon juice

- Place fish filets with a little butter in greased shallow pan and sprinkle with salt and pepper.
- Bake at 375° for about 8 to 10 minutes, turn and bake another 6 minutes or until fish flakes.
- For sauce, melt butter with tarragon, capers and lemon juice and serve over warm fish.

Crispy Baked Fish

3 to 4 fish filets, rinsed, dried
1 cup mayonnaise
2 tablespoons fresh lime juice and lime wedges
1½ cups crushed corn chips

- Preheat oven to 425°.
- Mix mayonnaise and lime juice and spread on both sides of fish filets.
- Place crushed corn chips on wax paper, dredge both sides of fish in chips and shake off excess chips.
- Place filets on foil-covered baking sheet and bake for 15 minutes or until fish flakes.
- Serve with lime wedges.

Catfish Amandine with a Kick!

¼ cup (½ stick) butter, melted
3 tablespoons lemon juice
6 to 8 catfish filets
1½ teaspoons Creole seasoning
½ cup sliced almonds

- Combine butter and lemon juice.
- Dip each filet in butter mixture, arrange in 9 x 13-inch baking dish and sprinkle fish with Creole seasoning.
- Bake at 375° for 25 to 30 minutes or until fish flakes easily when tested with fork.
- Sprinkle almonds over fish for last 5 minutes of baking.

Fish in Chips

2 pounds sole or orange roughy
½ cup caesar salad dressing
1 cup crushed potato chips
½ cup shredded cheddar cheese

- Dip fish in dressing and place in greased baking dish. · Combine potato chips and cheese and sprinkle over fish.
- Bake at 375° for about 20 to 25 minutes.

Pepper Orange Roughy

1 pound orange roughy filets
1 onion, sliced
2 red bell peppers, cut into julienne strips
1 teaspoon dried thyme leaves
¼ teaspoon black pepper

- Cut fish into 4 serving-size pieces.
- Heat a little oil in skillet, layer onion and bell peppers in oil and sprinkle with half thyme and pepper.
- Place fish over peppers and sprinkle with remaining thyme and pepper.
- Turn burner on high just until fish begins to cook.
- Lower heat, cover and cook fish for 15 to 20 minutes or until fish flakes easily.

Parmesan Flounder

⅓ cup mayonnaise
1 pound flounder filets
1 cup dry, seasoned breadcrumbs
¼ cup grated parmesan cheese

- Place mayonnaise in small dish.
- Coat fish with mayonnaise and dip in crumbs to coat well.
- Arrange in shallow baking dish and bake uncovered at 375° for 25 minutes.
- Add cheese!

Broiled Salmon Steaks

4 (1-inch thick) salmon steaks Garlic salt
Worcestershire sauce
¼ to ½ cup (½ to 1 stick) butter, melted

- Place salmon steaks on baking sheet and sprinkle both sides with garlic salt.
- Splash Worcestershire and butter on top of each steak and broil for 2 to 3 minutes.
- Remove from oven and turn each steak.
- Splash Worcestershire and butter over top and broil for 2 to 3 more minutes. (Do not overcook. Fish will flake but should not be dry inside.)
- Top with a little melted butter just before serving.

Salmon Patties

1 (15 ounce) can pink salmon with juice
1 egg
½ cup cracker crumbs
1 teaspoon baking powder

- Drain juice from salmon and set juice aside.
- Remove bones and skin from salmon.
- Combine egg and cracker crumbs with salmon.
- In small bowl, add baking powder to ¼ cup salmon juice. (Mixture will foam.)
- After foaming, add to salmon mixture and drop by teaspoonfuls into hot oil in skillet.
- Brown lightly on both sides and serve hot.

Salmon Croquets

1 (15 ounce) can pink salmon, drained, flaked

1 egg

½ cup biscuit mix

¼ cup ketchup

- Combine salmon (discard skin and bones) and egg in bowl.

- Add biscuit mix and ketchup and mix well.

- Heat a little oil in skillet and drop salmon mixture by tablespoonfuls into skillet.

- Flatten each croquet with spatula and cook each side until brown.

Tuna Pot Pie

1 (8 ounce) package crescent rolls, divided

1 (6 ounce) can solid white tuna in water, drained, flaked

1 (15 ounce) can cut asparagus, drained

1 cup shredded cheddar cheese

- Form 7-inch square using 4 crescent rolls, pinch edges together to seal and place in sprayed 8 x 8 x 2-inch baking pan.

- Spread dough with tuna, then asparagus, followed by shredded cheese.

- Form remaining 4 crescent rolls into 7-inch square and place on top of cheese.

- Bake at 375° for 20 minutes or until top is brown and cheese bubbles.

Classic Beer Batter Shrimp

1 (12 ounce) can beer
1 cup flour
2 teaspoons garlic powder
1 pound shrimp, peeled, veined

- Combine beer, flour and garlic powder and stir to creamy consistency to make batter.
- Dip shrimp into batter to cover and deep fry in hot oil.

Last-Minute Shrimp Scampi

½ cup (1 stick) butter
3 cloves garlic, pressed
¼ cup lemon juice
Hot sauce
2 pounds raw shrimp, peeled

- Melt butter, sauté garlic and add lemon juice and a few dashes of hot sauce.
- Arrange shrimp in single layer in shallow pan, pour butter mixture over shrimp and salt lightly.
- Broil 2 minutes, turn shrimp and broil 2 more minutes.
- Reserve garlic butter and serve separately.

This recipe requires real butter—no substitutions.

Zesty 6-Minute Shrimp

1 pound shrimp, peeled, veined
1 teaspoon garlic salt
2 tablespoons lemon juice
2 tablespoons (¼ stick) butter

- Place shrimp in shallow baking pan.
- Sprinkle with garlic salt and lemon juice and dot with butter.
- Broil on 1 side for 3 minutes, turn and broil 3 minutes more.

If shrimp are large, split them down the middle and butterfly them before seasoning.

Easy Crab Casserole

2 (6 ounce) cans crabmeat, drained
1 cup cream of mushroom soup
½ cup shredded Swiss cheese
½ cup seasoned breadcrumbs

- Combine crabmeat, soup and cheese and mix well.
- Pour into greased 1½-quart casserole dish and sprinkle with breadcrumbs.
- Bake uncovered at 350° for 30 minutes or until soup bubbles and breadcrumbs are brown.

Easy Fast Leftovers

Chicken or Turkey Salad

⅔ cup chopped celery
¾ cup sweet pickle relish
1 bunch fresh green onions with tops, chopped
3 hard-boiled eggs, chopped
¾ cup mayonnaise
3 cups cooked, cubed chicken or turkey

- Combine 3 cups chicken, celery, relish, onions and eggs.
- Toss with mayonnaise and chill.
- Serve on lettuce leaf.

Chicken or Turkey Salad

1 cup chopped celery
1 cup tart green apple, peeled, cubed
1 (11 ounce) can mandarin oranges, drained
¾ cup chopped macadamia nuts
1 teaspoon curry powder
¾ cup mayonnaise
3 cups cooked, cubed chicken or turkey

- Combine 3 cups chicken, celery, apple, oranges and nuts.
- Toss with curry powder and mayonnaise and chill.
- Serve on lettuce leaf.

Chicken or Turkey Salad

1 cup chopped celery

1½ cups halved green grapes

¾ cup cashew nuts

¾ cup mayonnaise

1 cup chow mein noodles

3 cups cooked, cubed chicken or turkey

- Combine 3 cups chicken, celery, grapes and cashew nuts and toss with mayonnaise.
- Just before serving, mix in noodles and serve on cabbage leaf.

Chicken or Turkey Salad

1 (6 ounce) box long-grain, wild rice, cooked, drained

1 bunch fresh green onions with tops, chopped

1 cup chopped walnuts

1 (8 ounce) can sliced water chestnuts

1 cup mayonnaise

¾ teaspoon curry powder

3 cups cooked, cubed chicken or turkey

- Combine 3 cups chicken, rice, onions, walnuts and water chestnuts.
- Toss with mayonnaise and curry powder and chill.
- Serve on bed of lettuce.

Chicken or Turkey Salad

⅔ cup chopped celery

1 (15 ounce) can pineapple tidbits, drained

¾ cup slivered almonds, toasted

¾ cup chopped red bell pepper

⅔ cup mayonnaise

3 cups cooked, cubed chicken or turkey

- Combine 3 cups chicken, celery, pineapple, almonds and bell pepper, toss with mayonnaise and chill.
- Serve on lettuce leaf.

Ranch-Style Turkey Pasta

1 (8 ounce) package pasta

½ cup (1 stick) butter

1 (1 ounce) packet dry ranch-style salad dressing mix

1 (15 ounce) can peas and carrots with liquid

3 cups cubed turkey or chicken

- Cook pasta according to directions on package.
- In saucepan, combine butter, dressing mix and peas and carrots and heat until butter melts.
- Toss with pasta and turkey and place in 2-quart casserole dish.
- Heat at 350° for about 20 minutes. (If you like, sprinkle some grated cheese over top after casserole bakes.)

Next Day Jambalaya

1 (15 ounce) can stewed tomatoes with liquid

1 (1 ounce) package dry vegetable soup/dip mix

¾ teaspoon crushed red pepper

2 cups chopped leftover chicken or turkey

1 cup ham, cut into julienne strips

- In large skillet, combine tomatoes, 2 cups water, soup mix and red pepper.
- Bring to a boil and stir well.
- Reduce heat, cover and simmer 15 minutes.
- Stir in chicken or turkey and ham, cook 5 minutes longer and serve over hot white rice.

Ham Salad

1 bunch fresh green onions with tops, chopped

½ cup slivered almonds, toasted

½ cup sunflower seeds

2 cups chopped fresh broccoli florets

¾ cup mayonnaise

3 cups cooked, chopped ham

- Combine 3 cups ham, green onions, almonds, sunflower seeds and broccoli florets, toss with mayonnaise and chill.
- Serve on lettuce leaf.

Ham Salad

¾ cup chopped celery
1 cup small-curd cottage cheese, drained
1 cup chopped cauliflower florets
1 cup chopped broccoli florets
Prepared honey mustard dressing
3 cups cooked, chopped ham

- Combine 3 cups ham, celery, cottage cheese, cauliflower and broccoli, toss with dressing and chill.
- Serve on lettuce leaves.

Ham 'n Cheese Mashed Potatoes

2 cups instant mashed potatoes
¾ teaspoon garlic powder
2 cups diced, cooked ham
1 (8 ounce) package shredded cheddar cheese
½ cup whipping cream

- In bowl, combine potatoes and garlic powder.
- Spread in buttered 2-quart baking dish and sprinkle with ham.
- Fold cheese into whipping cream and spoon over ham.
- Bake uncovered at 400° for 15 minutes or until golden brown.

Meat Drawer Spread

2 cups cooked ham or roast beef

¾ cup sweet pickle relish

2 celery ribs, finely chopped

2 hard-boiled eggs, chopped

½ onion, finely chopped Mayonnaise

- Chop meat in food processor, add relish, celery, eggs and onion and add a little salt and pepper.
- Fold in enough mayonnaise to make mixture spreadable and chill.
- Spread on crackers or bread for sandwiches.

Easy Fast
Desserts

Amaretto Ice Cream

1 (8 ounce) carton whipping cream, whipped
1 pint vanilla ice cream, softened
⅓ cup amaretto
⅓ cup chopped almonds, toasted

- Combine whipped cream, ice cream and amaretto and freeze in sherbet glasses.
- When ready to serve, drizzle a little additional amaretto over top of each individual serving and sprinkle with toasted almonds.

Divine Strawberries

1 quart fresh strawberries
1 (20 ounce) can pineapple chunks, well drained
2 bananas, sliced
1 (18 ounce) carton strawberry glaze

- Cut strawberries in half (or in quarters if strawberries are very large).
- Add pineapple chunks and bananas.
- Fold in strawberry glaze and chill.

This is wonderful over pound cake or just served in sherbet glasses.

Brandied Apples

1 (12 ounce) loaf pound cake
1 (20 ounce) can apple pie filling
$\frac{1}{2}$ teaspoon allspice
2 tablespoons brandy
Vanilla ice cream

- Slice pound cake and place on dessert plates.
- In saucepan, combine pie filling, allspice and brandy. Heat and stir just until heated thoroughly.
- Place several spoonfuls pie filling mixture over cake and top with scoop of vanilla ice cream.

Brandied Apple Topping

1 (20 ounce) can apple pie filling
$\frac{1}{4}$ teaspoon allspice
$\frac{1}{4}$ teaspoon cinnamon
$4\frac{1}{2}$ tablespoons brandy

- Pour apple pie filling onto dinner plate or into shallow bowl and cut apple slices into smaller chunks.
- Place pie filling, allspice, cinnamon and brandy in saucepan and cook over medium heat for 5 minutes.
- Pour topping over pound cake or vanilla ice cream.

Creamy Amaretto Toffee

1 (9 ounce) bag small chocolate-covered toffee candy bars, crumbled

30 caramels

$\frac{1}{3}$ cup amaretto liqueur

$\frac{1}{2}$ cup sour cream

1 cup whipping cream

- Reserve about $\frac{1}{3}$ cup crumbled toffee bars.
- In buttered 7 x 11-inch dish, spread remaining candy crumbs.
- In saucepan, melt caramels with amaretto and cool to room temperature.
- Stir in creams, whip until thick and pour into individual dessert dishes.
- Top with reserved candy crumbs, cover and freeze.

Snickers Surprise

3 (2.07 ounce) Snickers candy bars, frozen

2 Granny Smith apples, chopped

1 (12 ounce) carton whipped topping

1 (3.4 ounce) package dry instant vanilla pudding mix

- Smash frozen candy bars in wrappers with hammer.
- Combine all ingredients and mix well. Chill.

Place in a pretty crystal bowl or serve in individual sherbet glasses.

Grasshopper Dessert

26 chocolate sandwich cookies, crushed
¼ cup (½ stick) butter, melted
¼ cup crème de menthe liqueur
2 (7 ounce) jars marshmallow cream
2 (8 ounce) cartons whipping cream

- Reserve about ⅓ cup crumbs for topping.
- Combine remaining cookie crumbs and butter and press into bottom of greased 9-inch springform pan.
- Gradually add crème de menthe to marshmallow cream.
- Whip cream until very thick and fold into marshmallow cream mixture. Pour over crumbs in pan.
- Sprinkle reserved cookie crumbs on top and freeze.

Coffee Creamy

3 cups miniature marshmallows
½ cup hot, strong coffee
1 cup whipping cream, whipped
½ teaspoon vanilla extract

- In large saucepan, combine marshmallows and coffee.
- On low heat, stir constantly and cook until marshmallows melt. Cool mixture.
- Fold in whipped cream and vanilla and stir until ready to serve.
- Pour into individual dessert glasses.

Wake Up and Smell the Desert

This is a super dessert—no slicing, no "dishing up"—just bring it right from the fridge to the table.

1 cup strong coffee
1 (10 ounce) package large marshmallows
1 (8 ounce) package chopped dates
1¼ cups chopped pecans
1 (8 ounce) carton whipping cream, whipped

- Melt marshmallows in hot coffee.
- Add dates and pecans and chill.
- When mixture thickens, fold in whipped cream.
- Pour into sherbet glasses. Place plastic wrap over top and chill.

Kahlua Mousse

Light but rich and absolutely delicious!

1 (12 ounce) carton whipped topping
2 teaspoons dry instant coffee granules
5 teaspoons cocoa
5 tablespoons sugar
½ cup kahlua liqueur

- In large bowl, combine whipped topping, coffee, cocoa and sugar and blend well.
- Fold in kahlua and spoon into sherbet dessert glasses.
- Place plastic wrap over dessert glasses until ready to serve.

Classic Banana Pudding

This is a quick and easy way to make the old favorite banana pudding.

1 (14 ounce) can sweetened condensed milk
1 (3.4 ounce) package instant vanilla pudding mix
1 (8 ounce) carton whipped topping
36 vanilla wafers
3 bananas

- In large bowl, combine condensed milk and 1½ cups cold water.
- Add pudding mix and beat well.
- Chill 5 minutes then fold in whipped topping.
- Spoon 1 cup pudding mixture into 3-quart glass serving bowl. Top with wafers, bananas and pudding. Repeat layers twice and end with pudding.
- Cover and refrigerate.

Peach Sundaes

1 pint vanilla ice cream
¾ cup peach preserves, warmed
¼ cup chopped almonds, toasted
¼ cup flaked coconut

- Divide ice cream into 4 sherbet dishes.
- Top with preserves.
- Sprinkle with almonds and coconut.

Caribbean Cream

2 soft mangoes
½ gallon vanilla ice cream, softened
1 (6 ounce) can frozen lemonade concentrate, thawed
1 (8 ounce) carton whipped topping

- Peel mangoes, cut slices around seeds and cut into small chunks.
- In large bowl, mix ice cream, lemonade and whipped topping and fold in mango chunks.
- Quickly spoon mixture into parfait or sherbet glasses and cover with plastic wrap.
- Place in freezer.

Peanut Butter Sundae

1 cup light corn syrup
1 cup chunky peanut butter
¼ cup milk
Ice cream or pound cake

- In mixing bowl, stir corn syrup, peanut butter and milk until they blend well.
- Serve over ice cream or pound cake.
- Store in refrigerator.

Dimestore Dessert

1 (10 count) box twinkies
4 bananas, sliced
1 (5 ounce) package vanilla instant pudding mix
1 (20 ounce) can crushed pineapple, drained
1 (8 ounce) carton whipped topping

- Slice twinkies in half lengthwise and place in buttered 9 x 13-inch pan cream side up.
- Make layer of sliced bananas.
- Prepare pudding according to package directions (use 2 cups milk).
- Pour over bananas and add pineapple.
- Top with whipped topping and refrigerate.
- Cut into squares to serve.

Easy Fast
Cakes

Pineapple Coconut Delight

1 (14 ounce) bakery pound cake
1 (20 ounce) can crushed pineapple with juice
1 (3.4 ounce) package instant coconut cream pudding mix
1 (8 ounce) carton whipped topping
½ cup flaked coconut

- Slice cake horizontally into 3 equal layers.
- Mix pineapple, pudding mix and whipped topping and blend well.
- Spread on each cake layer and over top.
- Sprinkle top of cake with coconut and chill.

St. Patrick's Cake

1 (14 ounce) pound cake loaf
1 (15 ounce) can crushed pineapple with juice
1 (3.4 ounce) package pistachio pudding mix
1 (8 ounce) carton whipped topping

- Slice cake horizontally into 3 equal layers.
- Combine pineapple and pudding mix and beat until mixture begins to thicken.
- Fold in whipped topping and blend well. (You may add a few drops of green food coloring if you would like the cake to be a brighter green.)
- Spread pineapple mixture on each cake layer and on top. Chill.

Pineapple-Crush Cake

1 bakery orange-chiffon cake
1 (15 ounce) can crushed pineapple with juice
1 (3.4 ounce) package vanilla instant pudding mix
1 (8 ounce) carton whipped topping
½ cup slivered almonds, toasted

- Slice cake horizontally into 3 equal layers.
- Mix pineapple, pudding mix and whipped topping and blend well.
- Spread pineapple mixture on each cake layer and cover top of cake. Sprinkle almonds on top and chill.

Coconut Layer Cake

1 (14 ounce) round angel food cake
1 (20 ounce) can coconut pie filling
1 (12 ounce) carton whipped topping
3 tablespoons flaked coconut

- Cut angel food cake horizontally into 3 equal layers.
- Combine coconut pie filling and whipped topping.
- Spread one-third of mixture on first layer and top with second layer.
- Spread one-third mixture on second layer and top with third layer.
- Spread remaining whipped topping mixture on top of cake and sprinkle with coconut.
- Chill.

Too Easy Pineapple Cake

2 cups sugar

2 cups flour

1 (20 ounce) can crushed pineapple with juice

1 teaspoon baking soda

- Preheat oven to 350°.
- Combine all cake ingredients and mix by hand.
- Pour into greased, floured 9 x 13-inch baking pan.
- Bake for 30 to 35 minutes.

Too Easy Pineapple Cake Icing:

1 (8 ounce) package cream cheese, softened

½ cup (1 stick) butter, melted

1 cup powdered sugar

1 cup chopped pecans

- Combine cream cheese, butter and powdered sugar and beat with mixer.
- Add chopped pecans and pour over hot cake.

Pink Ice Pie

½ gallon vanilla ice cream, softened

1 (6 ounce) can frozen pink lemonade concentrate

1 (9 inch) graham cracker piecrust

- With mixer, combine ice cream and lemonade concentrate. (Work quickly.)
- Pile ice cream mixture in piecrust and freeze.

Lemon-Pineapple Cake

1 (18 ounce) box lemon cake mix

1 (20 ounce) can crushed pineapple with juice

3 eggs

⅓ cup oil

- Preheat oven to 350°.
- In mixing bowl, combine all cake ingredients. Blend on low speed to moisten and beat on medium for 2 minutes.
- Pour batter into greased, floured 9 x 13-inch baking pan.
- Bake for 30 minutes. Test with toothpick to be sure cake is done. (While cake is baking, prepare topping for cake.) Cool for 15 minutes.

Lemon-Pineapple Cake Topping:

1 (14 ounce) can sweetened condensed milk

1 cup sour cream

¼ cup lemon juice

- In medium bowl, combine all topping ingredients. Stir well to blend.
- Pour over warm cake. Chill.

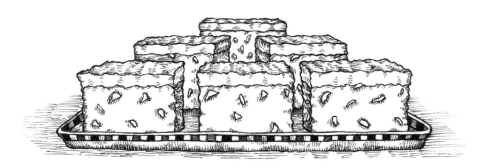

Strawberry with Wings Cake

1 cup sweetened condensed milk
¼ cup lemon juice
1 pint fresh strawberries, halved
1 (14 ounce) angel food cake
1 pint whipping cream, whipped

- Combine condensed milk and lemon juice and fold in strawberries.
- Slice cake in half.
- Spread strawberry filling on bottom layer and place top layer over filling.
- Cover with whipped cream and top with extra strawberries.

Zesty Chocolate Cake

1 (16 ounce) loaf frozen pound cake, thawed
1 (12 ounce) jar orange marmalade
1 (16 ounce) can ready-to-spread chocolate-fudge frosting

- Cut cake horizontally into 3 equal layers.
- Place 1 layer on cake platter and spread with half marmalade.
- Place second layer over first and spread with remaining marmalade.
- Top with third cake layer and spread frosting liberally on top and sides of cake.
- Chill.

Easy Fast
Pies
and
Cobblers

Last Minute Party Pies

Eat one and freeze the other!

1 (14 ounce) can sweetened condensed milk
1 (20 ounce) can lemon pie filling
1 (20 ounce) can crushed pineapple, well drained
1 (8 ounce) carton whipped topping
2 (9 inch) cookie-flavored piecrusts

- With mixer, combine condensed milk and lemon pie filling and beat until smooth.
- Gently fold pineapple and whipped topping into pie filling mixture.
- Pour into 2 piecrusts and refrigerate.

Bye Bye Strawberry Pie

2 pints fresh strawberries, divided
1¼ cups sugar
3 tablespoons cornstarch
1 (9 inch) graham cracker piecrust
1 (8 ounce) carton whipping cream, whipped

- Crush 1 pint strawberries, add sugar, cornstarch and a dash of salt and cook on low heat until thick and clear. Cool.
- Place other pint of strawberries in piecrust and cover with cooked mixture.
- Top with whipping cream and refrigerate.

Strawberry-Cream Cheese Pie

2 (10 ounce) packages frozen sweetened strawberries, thawed

2 (8 ounce) packages cream cheese, softened

⅔ cup powdered sugar

1 (8 ounce) carton whipped topping

1 (9 inch) prepared chocolate crumb piecrust

- Drain strawberries and reserve ¼ cup juice.

- In mixing bowl, combine cream cheese, reserved juice, strawberries and sugar and beat well.

- Fold in whipped topping and spoon into piecrust.

- Refrigerate overnight and garnish with fresh strawberries.

Thanksgiving Anytime Pie

1 (6 ounce) package strawberry gelatin mix

1 cup whole cranberry sauce

½ cup cranberry juice cocktail

1 (8 ounce) carton whipped topping

1 (9 inch) baked piecrust

- Dissolve gelatin in 1 cup boiling water. Add cranberry sauce and juice and chill until it begins to thicken.

- Fold in whipped topping, chill again until mixture mounds and pour into piecrust.

- Refrigerate several hours before serving.

Gold 'n Fluffy Pie

24 round, buttery crackers, crumbled
1 cup chopped pecans
4 egg whites (absolutely no yolks at all)
1 cup sugar

- Preheat oven to 350°.
- In bowl, combine cracker crumbs with pecans.
- In separate mixing bowl, beat egg whites until stiff and slowly add sugar while still mixing.
- Gently fold crumb mixture into egg whites.
- Pour into 9 inch pie pan, bake for 20 minutes and cool before serving.

Mother-in-Law Pie

Impress even your mother-in-law with this easy delicious dessert!

1 (8 ounce) package cream cheese, softened
1 (14 ounce) can sweetened condensed milk
1 (3.4 ounce) package instant vanilla pudding mix
1½ cups whipped topping
1 (9 inch) prepared graham cracker piecrust

- Use mixer to beat cream cheese until smooth. Gradually add condensed milk and beat until smooth.
- Add ¾ cup water and pudding mix and beat until smooth.
- Fold in whipped topping and pour into piecrust.
- Top with crumbled holiday candies and chill.

Mintmallow Pie

22 large marshmallows
$\frac{1}{3}$ cup crème de menthe
1 (12 ounce) carton whipping cream, whipped
1 (9 inch) prepared chocolate piecrust

- In large saucepan, melt marshmallows with crème de menthe over low heat and cool.
- Fold whipped cream into marshmallow mixture.
- Pour filling into piecrust and freeze until ready to serve.

Luau Pie

$\frac{1}{2}$ gallon vanilla ice cream, softened
$\frac{1}{3}$ cup plus
1 tablespoon kahlua
$\frac{1}{3}$ cup plus
1 tablespoon amaretto
1 (9 inch) prepared chocolate cookie crust
$\frac{1}{4}$ cup slivered almonds, toasted

- Place ice cream, kahlua and amaretto in mixing bowl and blend as quickly as possible.
- Pour into piecrust, sprinkle almonds over top and freeze.

Creamy Chocolate Pie

1 (8 ounce) package cream cheese, softened
¾ cup powdered sugar
¼ cup cocoa
1 (8 ounce) container whipped topping, thawed
½ cup chopped pecans
1 (9 inch) prepared crumb piecrust

- Combine cream cheese, sugar and cocoa in mixing bowl and beat at medium speed until creamy.
- Add whipped topping and fold until smooth.
- Spread into piecrust, sprinkle pecans over top and refrigerate.

Key Lime Pie

6 egg yolks
2 (14 ounce) cans sweetened condensed milk
1 (8 ounce) bottle lime juice from concentrate
1 (9 inch) graham cracker piecrust

- Preheat oven to 350°.
- In large mixing bowl, beat egg yolks with condensed milk.
- Stir in lime juice and green food coloring if you like.
- Pour mixture into piecrust and bake for 20 minutes.
- Chill. Top with whipped cream.

Cherry Cobbler Rolls

1 (20 ounce) can cherry pie filling
1 (12 ounce) tube refrigerated cinnamon rolls

- Preheat oven to 400°.
- Spread pie filling into greased 8-inch baking dish.
- Set aside icing from cinnamon rolls and arrange rolls around edge of baking dish.
- Bake for 15 minutes. Cover and bake 10 minutes longer.
- Spread icing over rolls and serve warm.

Easy Fast
Cookies

Easy Peanut Butter Cookies

1 (18 ounce) package sugar cookie dough
½ cup creamy peanut butter
½ cup miniature chocolate chips
½ cup peanut butter chips
½ cup chopped peanuts

- Preheat oven to 350°.
- Beat cookie dough and peanut butter in large bowl until blended and smooth.
- Stir in chocolate chips, peanut butter chips and peanuts and mix well.
- Drop dough by heaping tablespoonfuls onto ungreased baking sheet.
- Bake for 15 minutes and cool on wire rack.

Butter Cookies

1 pound butter
¾ cup packed brown sugar
¾ cup granulated sugar
4½ cups flour

- Preheat oven to 350°.
- Cream butter and sugars, slowly add flour and mix well. (Batter will be very thick.)
- Roll into small balls and place on ungreased baking sheet.
- Bake for about 15 minutes until only slightly brown. Do not overbake.

Cheesecake Cookies

1 cup (2 sticks) butter, softened
2 (3 ounce) packages cream cheese, softened
2 cups sugar
2 cups flour

- Preheat oven to 350°.
- Cream butter and cream cheese, add sugar and beat until light and fluffy. Add flour and beat well.
- Drop by teaspoonfuls onto baking sheet and bake for 12 to 15 minutes or until edges are golden.

These are even better if you add 1 cup chopped pecans.

Cocoa-Nut Cookies

1 cup sweetened condensed milk
4 cups flaked coconut
$2/3$ cup miniature semi-sweet chocolate bits
1 teaspoon vanilla extract
$1/2$ teaspoon almond extract

- Preheat oven to 325°.
- Combine milk and coconut. (Mixture will be gooey.)
- Add chocolate bits and extracts and stir until well blended.
- Drop by teaspoonfuls onto sprayed baking sheet and bake for 12 minutes.
- Store in airtight container.

Coconut Macaroons

2 (7 ounce) packages flaked coconut

1 (14 ounce) can sweetened condensed milk

2 teaspoons vanilla extract

$\frac{1}{2}$ teaspoon almond extract

- Preheat oven to 350°.
- In mixing bowl, combine coconut, condensed milk and extracts and mix well.
- Drop by rounded teaspoons onto foil-lined baking sheet.
- Bake for 8 to 10 minutes or until light brown around edges.
- Immediately remove from foil. (Macaroons will stick if allowed to cool.) Store at room temperature.

Choconut Squares

$1\frac{1}{2}$ cups graham cracker crumbs

1 (6 ounce) package chocolate chips

1 cup flaked coconut

$1\frac{1}{4}$ cups chopped pecans

1 (14 ounce) can sweetened condensed milk

- Preheat oven to 350°.
- Sprinkle cracker crumbs in 9 x 9-inch pan.
- Layer chocolate chips, coconut and pecans and pour condensed milk over top of layered ingredients.
- Bake for 25 to 30 minutes. Cool and cut into squares.

Lemon Drops

½ (8 ounce) carton whipped topping

1 (18 ounce) box lemon cake mix

1 egg

Powdered sugar

- Preheat oven to 350°.
- Stir whipped topping into lemon cake mix by hand, add egg and mix thoroughly.
- Shape dough into balls and roll in powdered sugar
- Bake for 8 to 10 minutes. Do not overcook.

Potato Chip Crunchies

These are really good and crunchy!

1 cup (2 sticks) butter, softened

⅔ cup sugar

1 teaspoon vanilla extract

1½ cups flour

½ cup crushed potato chips

- Preheat oven to 350°.
- Cream butter, sugar and vanilla. Add flour and chips and mix well.
- Drop by teaspoonfuls on ungreased baking sheet.
- Bake for about 12 minutes or until light brown.

Butter Tarts

1 cup (2 sticks) butter, softened
¾ cup powdered sugar
2 cups sifted flour
1 cup chopped pecans
1 teaspoon vanilla extract

- Preheat oven to 325°.
- With mixer, cream butter and sugar and add flour, pecans and vanilla.
- Roll into crescents and place on ungreased baking sheet.
- Bake for 20 minutes and roll in extra powdered sugar after tarts cool.

Pumpkin Cupcakes

1 (18 ounce) box spice cake mix
1 (15 ounce) can pumpkin
3 eggs
⅓ cup oil
⅓ cup water

- Preheat oven to 350°.
- With mixer, blend all ingredients and beat for 2 minutes.
- Pour batter into 24 paper-lined muffin cups and fill three-fourths full.
- Bake for 18 to 20 minutes or until toothpick inserted in center comes out clean. (You might want to spread with commercial icing.)

Citrus Balls

1 (12 ounce) box vanilla wafers, crushed

½ cup (1 stick) butter, melted

1 (16 ounce) box powdered sugar

1 (6 ounce) can frozen orange juice concentrate

1 cup finely chopped pecans

- Combine wafer crumbs, butter, sugar and orange juice concentrate and mix well.
- Form into balls, roll in chopped pecans and store in airtight container.

Make these in finger shapes for something different. They make neat cookies for a party or a tea.

Soft 'n Crispy Treats

¼ cup (½ stick) butter

4 cups miniature marshmallows

½ cup chunky peanut butter

5 cups crispy rice cereal

- In saucepan, melt butter. Add marshmallows, stir until they melt and add peanut butter.
- Remove from heat. Add cereal and stir well.
- Press mixture into 9 x 13-inch pan. Cut in squares when cool.

Haystacks

1 (12 ounce) package butterscotch chips
1 cup salted peanuts
1½ cups chow mein noodles

- Melt butterscotch chips in top of double boiler.
- Remove from heat and stir in peanuts and noodles.
- Drop by teaspoonfuls on wax paper.
- Cool and store in airtight container.

Choco-Crunch Bars

1 (20 ounce) package chocolate
¾ cup light corn syrup
2 tablespoons (¼ stick) butter
2 teaspoons vanilla extract
8 cups crispy rice cereal

- Combine chocolate, corn syrup and butter in top of double boiler.
- Heat on low and cook until chocolate melts. Remove from heat and stir in vanilla.
- Place cereal in large mixing bowl, pour chocolate mixture on top and stir until well coated.
- Quickly spoon mixture into buttered 9 x 13-inch dish and press firmly, using back of spoon.
- Cool completely and cut into bars.

Butternoodles

1 (12 ounce) and 1 (6 ounce) package butterscotch chips
2¼ cups chow mein noodles
½ cup chopped walnuts
¼ cup flaked coconut

- Melt butterscotch chips in double boiler. Add noodles, walnuts and coconut.
- Drop by tablespoonfuls onto wax paper.

Coconut Cookie Bars

½ cup (1 stick) butter
2 cups graham cracker crumbs
1 (14 ounce) can sweetened condensed milk
⅔ cup flaked coconut
1 cup chopped pecans
1 cup M&Ms plain chocolate candies

- Preheat oven to 350°.
- In 9 x 13-inch baking pan, melt butter in oven.
- Sprinkle crumbs over butter and pour condensed milk over crumbs.
- Top with coconut, pecans and M&Ms and press down firmly.
- Bake for 25 to 30 minutes or until light brown. Cool and cut into bars.

When making these one time, I realized I was missing the M&Ms, so I substituted white chocolate bits. They were great.

Honey Bunches of Chocolate

⅓ cup (⅔ stick) butter

¼ cup cocoa

1 (10 ounce) package miniature marshmallows

6 cups honey-nut clusters cereal

- Melt butter in large saucepan and stir in cocoa and marshmallows.
- Cook over low heat, stirring constantly, until marshmallows melt and mixture is smooth.
- Remove from heat and stir in cereal.
- Pour into sprayed 7 x 11-inch pan and smooth mixture with spatula.
- Cool completely and cut into bars.

Kids' Krispies

1 cup sugar

1 cup light corn syrup

1½ cups crunchy peanut butter

6 cups crispy rice cereal

1 (12 ounce) package chocolate chips

- In saucepan, combine sugar and corn syrup and bring to a boil, stirring constantly.
- Remove from heat and stir in peanut butter and crispy rice cereal. Spread into buttered 9 x 13-inch pan.
- In saucepan over low heat, melt chocolate chips and spread over cereal layer.
- Refrigerate until set and cut into bars. Store in refrigerator.

Apricot Squares

1¼ cups flour

¾ cup packed brown sugar

6 tablespoons (¾ stick) butter

¾ cup apricot preserves

- Preheat oven to 350°.

- In mixing bowl, combine flour, brown sugar and butter and mix well.

- Place half mixture in 9-inch square baking pan, spread apricot preserves over top and sprinkle with remaining flour mixture.

- Bake for 30 minutes. Cut into squares.

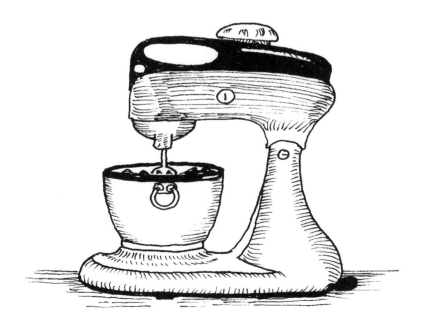

Easy Fast Candies

Platinum Fudge

1 (6 ounce) package semi-sweet chocolate morsels
1 cup creamy peanut butter
½ cup (1 stick) butter
1 cup powdered sugar

- Combine morsels, peanut butter and butter in saucepan over low heat. Stir constantly, just until mixture melts and is smooth.

- Remove from heat, add powdered sugar and stir until smooth.

- Spoon into buttered 8-inch square pan and chill until firm.

- Let stand 10 minutes at room temperature before cutting into squares and store in refrigerator.

Creamy White Fudge

1 (8 ounce) package cream cheese, softened
4 cups powdered sugar
1½ teaspoons vanilla extract
12 ounces almond bark, melted
¾ cup chopped pecans

- Beat cream cheese at medium speed with mixer until smooth, gradually add sugar and vanilla and beat well.

- Stir in melted almond bark and pecans and spread into buttered 8-inch square pan.

- Refrigerate until firm and cut into small squares.

This is a little different slant to fudge—really creamy and really good!

Mocha-Butter Drops

1 cup sugar

½ cup light corn syrup

¼ cup honey

1 (12 ounce) jar chunky peanut butter

4 cups chocolate-flavored frosted corn puff cereal

- Combine sugar, corn syrup and honey in Dutch oven. Bring to boil and stir constantly.
- Remove from heat, add peanut butter and stir until it blends.
- Stir in cereal and drop by tablespoonfuls onto wax paper.
- Let cool.

Handy Candy

2 (8 ounce) cartons whipping cream

3 cups sugar

1 cup light corn syrup

1 cup chopped pecans

- In saucepan, combine whipping cream, sugar and corn syrup and cook to soft-ball stage (234° on candy thermometer).
- Stir and beat until candy is cool.
- Add pecans and pour into buttered 9-inch pan.

21st Century Pralines

1½ cups packed brown sugar

⅔ cup half-and-half cream

Dash of salt

2 tablespoons (¼ stick) butter, melted

1⅔ cups chopped pecans

- Combine brown sugar, cream and salt in deep glass dish and mix well. Blend in butter.
- Microwave on HIGH for 10 minutes, stir once and add pecans. Cool for 1 minute.
- Beat by hand until creamy and thick, about 4 to 5 minutes. (The mixture will lose some of its gloss.)
- Drop by tablespoonfuls onto wax paper.

Cocoa-Butter Puffs

¾ cup light corn syrup

1¼ cups sugar

1¼ cups chunky peanut butter

4½ cups cocoa puff cereal

- In large saucepan, bring syrup and sugar to rolling boil.
- Stir in peanut butter and mix well. Stir in cocoa puffs and drop on wax paper by teaspoonfuls.

Orangy Haystacks

1 pound candy orange slices, chopped
2 cups flaked coconut
2 cups chopped pecans
1 (14 ounce) can sweetened condensed milk
2 cups powdered sugar

- Place orange slices, coconut, pecans and condensed milk in baking dish and cook at 350° for 12 minutes or until bubbly.
- Add powdered sugar and mix well.
- Drop by teaspoonfuls on wax paper.

Pralines in Minutes

1 (3 ounce) box butterscotch cook-and-serve pudding mix
1¼ cups sugar
½ cup evaporated milk
2 cups pecan pieces

- In large saucepan, mix butterscotch pudding mix, sugar and milk.
- Bring to a boil and stir constantly for 2 minutes.
- Add pecans, boil another 1½ minutes and stir constantly.
- Remove from heat and beat until candy begins to cool.

Peanut Krispies

¾ cup (1½ sticks) butter

2 cups peanut butter

1 (16 ounce) box powdered sugar

3½ cups crispy rice cereal

¾ cup chopped peanuts

- Melt butter in large saucepan, add peanut butter and mix well.
- Add powdered sugar, cereal and peanuts and mix.
- Drop by teaspoonfuls on wax paper.

U.S. Measurement and Metric Conversion Charts

3 teaspoons = 1 tablespoon

2 cups = 1 pint

2 pints = 1 quart

4 quarts = 1 gallon

8 cups = 64 oz. = ½ gallon = 2 quarts = 1.9 liter

16 cups = 1 gallon = 4 quarts = 3.8 liter

2 gallons = 8 quarts = 7.6 liter

Teaspoons	
⅛ teaspoon	5 ml
¼ teaspoon	1 ml
½ teaspoon	2 ml
⅓ teaspoon	3 ml
⅔ teaspoon	3 ml
¾ teaspoon	4 ml
1 teaspoon	5 ml
1½ teaspoons	7 ml
1¾ teaspoons	9 ml
2 teaspoons	10 ml
3 teaspoons	15 ml
4 teaspoons	20 ml
5 teaspoons	25 ml

Tablespoons	
½ tablespoon	7 ml
1 tablespoon	15 ml
1½ tablespoons	22 ml
2 tablespoons	30 ml
3 tablespoons	45 ml
4 tablespoons	60 ml
5 tablespoons	75 ml
6 tablespoons	90 ml
8 tablespoons	105 ml

● ●

Volume & Liquid Measure

¼ cup	60 ml	3 cups	710 ml
⅓ cup	80 ml	3¼ cups	770 ml
½ cup	120 ml	3⅓ cups	790 ml
⅔ cup	160 ml	3½ cups	830 ml
¾ cup	180 ml	3⅔ cups	870 ml
1 cup	240 ml	3¾ cups	890 ml
1¼ cups	300 ml	4 cups=32 oz=1 qt.	960 ml
1⅓ cups	320 ml	4 ¾ cups	1.1 L
1½ cups	360 ml	5 cups	1.3 L
1⅔ cups	400 ml	6 cups=48 oz=1½ qt.	1.5 L
1¾ cups	420 ml	7 cups	1.6 L
2 cups=1 pint	480 ml	8 cups=2 qts.	1.8 L
2¼ cups	540 ml	9 cups	(2 L)
2⅓ cups	560 ml	10 cups	(2.5 L)
2½ cups	600 ml	12 cups	(3 L)
2⅔ cups	640 ml	1 gallon=4 quarts	3.8 L
2¾ cups	660 ml	2 gallons=8 quarts	7.6 L

Quarts

1 quart	1 liters
2-quarts	2 liters
2½-quarts	2.5 liters
3-quarts	3 liters
3½-quarts	3.5 liters
4-quarts	4 liters

Weights

.03 ounce	10 g	20 ounces	567 g
½ ounce	14 g	22 ounces	624 g
¾ ounce	21 g	24 ounces	681 g
1 ounce	28 g	25 ounces	708 g
1.25 ounces	38 g	28 ounces	794 g
1.3 ounces	40 g	29 ounces	805 g
1.5 ounces	42 g	32 ounces	1 kg
2 ounces	57 g	36 ounces	1.1 kg
2.25 ounces	64 g	38 ounces	1.1 kg
2.5 ounces	70 g	40 ounces	1.15 kg
3 ounces	84 g	42 ounces	1.2 kg
3.5 ounces	100 g	44 ounces	1.25 kg
4 ounces	114 g	46 ounces	1.3 kg
4.5 ounces	128 g	48 ounces	1.3 kg
5 ounces	143 g	52 ounces	1.4 kg
5.5 ounces	154 g	64 ounces	2 kg
6 ounces	168 g		
7 ounces	196 g	¼ pound	114 g
8 ounces	227 g	⅓ pound	150 g
9 ounces	252 g	½ pound	227 g
10 ounces	280 g	¾ pound	340 g
11 ounces	312 g	1 pound	454 g (.5 kg)
12 ounces	340 g	1¼ pounds	567 g
13 ounces	370 g	1½ pounds	680 g (.7 kg)
14 ounces	396 g	2 pounds	908 g (1 kg)
15 ounces	425 g	2½ pounds	(1.2 kg)
16 ounces	454 g	3 pounds	(1.5 kg)
17 ounces	484 g	4 pounds	(2 kg)
18 ounces	510 g	5 pounds	(2.5 kg)
19 ounces	538 g	6 pounds	(3 kg)
		8 pounds	(4 kg)

Temperatures

°F	°C
160°	71°
180°	82°
200°	93°
240°	125°
250°	121°
275°	135°
300°	148°
325°	162°
350°	176°
375°	190°
400°	204°
425°	220°
450°	230°
475°	250°
500°	260°

U.S. Measurements & Food Equivalents

3 teaspoons	1 tablespoon	
4 tablespoons	¼ cup	2 fluid ounces
8 tablespoons	½ cup	4 fluid ounces
12 tablespoons	¾ cup	6 fluid ounces
16 tablespoons	1 cup	8 fluid ounces
¼ cup	4 tablespoons	2 fluid ounces
⅓ cup	5 tablespoons + 1 teaspoons	
½ cup	8 tablespoons	4 fluid ounces
⅔ cup	10 tablespoons + 2 teaspoons	
¾ cup	12 tablespoons	6 fluid ounces
1 cup	16 tablespoons	8 fluid ounces
1 cup	½ pint	
2 cups	1 pint	16 fluid ounces
3 cups	1½ pints	24 fluid ounces
4 cups	1 quart	32 fluid ounces
8 cups	2 quarts	64 fluid ounces
1 pint	2 cups	16 fluid ounces
2 pints	1 quart	
1 quart	2 pints; 4 cups	32 fluid ounces
4 quarts	1 gallon; 8 pints; 16 cups	
8 quarts	1 peck	
4 pecks	1 bushel	

Cake Pans

5 x 2 round	2⅔ cups
6 x 2 round	3¾ cups
8 x 1.5 round	4 cups
7 x 2 round	5¼ cups
8 x 2 round	6 cups
9 x 1.5 round	6 cups
9 x 2 round	8 cups
9 x 3 bundt	9 cups
10 x 3.5 bundt	12 cups
9.5 x 2.5 springform ...	10 cups
10 x 2.5 springform ...	12 cups
8 x 3 tube	9 cups
9 x 4 tube	11 cups
10 x 4 tube	16 cups

Casseroles

8 x 8 x12 square	8 cups
11 x7 x 12 rectangular ...	8 cups
9 x9 x 2 square	10 cups
13 x 9 x 2 rectangular	15 cups
1-quart casserole	4 cups
2-quart casserole	8 cups
2.5 quart casserole	10 cups
3-quart casserole	12 cups

Ingredient Equivalents

Food	Amount	Approximate Equivalent
Apples	1 pound fresh	3 medium; 2¼ cups chopped; 3 cups sliced
Bacon	1 slice, cooked	1 tbsp. crumbled
Bread	1 (1 pound) loaf	14–18 regular slices; 7 cups crumbs ½ cup crumbs
Breadcrumbs	1 (8 ounce) pkg.	2⅓ cups
Breadcrumbs, dry	1 cup	¾ cup cracker crumbs
Broccoli	1 pound fresh	2 cups chopped
Broth, chicken or beef	1 cup	1 bouillon cube; 1 tsp. granules in 1 cup boiling water
Butter	1 pound regular 1 stick 1 cup (4 ounces)	4 sticks; 2 cups; ½ cup; 8 tbsp. ⅞ cup vegetable oil or shortening; 1 cup margarine
Buttermilk	1 cup	1 tbsp. lemon juice or white vinegar plus milk to equal 1 cup (must stand for 5 minutes)
Celery	2 ribs	½ cup chopped
Cottage Cheese	1 cup	1 cup ricotta
Crackers	15 graham crackers 28 saltine crackers	1 cup crumbs 1 cup crumbs
Cream	½ pint light ½ pint whipping ½ pint sour cream	1 cup 1 cup; 2 cups whipped 1 cup
Cream Cheese	8 ounces	1 cup
Chicken	3–3½ pounds 1 whole breast	3 cups cooked meat 1½ cups cooked, chopped
Chocolate	6 ounce chips	1 cup
Chocolate wafers	18–20 cookies	1 cup crumbs
Cornstarch	1 tbsp.	2 tbsp. flour
Cream, whipping	1 cup	4 ounces frozen whipped topping

Food	Amount	Approximate Equivalent
Flour	1 cup sifted all-purpose	1 cup minus 2 tbsp. unsifted all-purpose
	1 cup sifted self-rising	1 cup sifted all-purpose flour plus 1½ tsp. baking powder plus ⅛ tsp. salt
Garlic	1 small clove	⅛ tsp. garlic powder
Grits	1 pound	3 cups
Ham	½ pound boneless	1½ cups chopped
Herbs	1 tbsp. fresh	1 tsp. dried
Honey	1 cup	1¼ cups granulated sugar plus ⅓ cup liquid in recipe
Ketchup	½ cup	½ cup tomato sauce plus 2 tbsp. sugar plus 1 tbsp. vinegar
Lemon juice	1 tsp.	½ tsp. vinegar
Lemons	4 - 6	1 cup juice
Limes	6 - 8	¾ cup juice
Macaroni	8 ounces	4 cups cooked
	1 cup	1¾ cups cooked
Marshmallows	6–7 large	1 cup
	85 miniature	1 cup
Milk	1 quart	4 cups
Milk, evaporated	5 ounce can	⅔ cup
Mushrooms	½ pound fresh	1 (6 ounce) can, drained
	1 pound	5 cups sliced; 6 cups chopped
Mustard	1 tbsp. prepared	1 tsp. dry
Oil	1 quart	4 cups
Onions	1 small	1 tbsp. instant minced; ½ tbsp. onion powder
Onions, green	5 bulbs only	½ cup chopped
	5 with tops	1¾ cups chopped
Onions, white	4 medium	3½ cups chopped
Oreo	22 cookies	1½ cups crumbs
Peaches	4 medium	2½ cups chopped or sliced
Peanut Butter	18 ounce jar	1¾ cups
Pecans	1 pound shelled	4 cups chopped

Food	Amount	Approximate Equivalent
Peppers, bell	2 large	2½ cups chopped; 3 cups sliced
	1 medium	1 cup chopped
Potatoes, sweet	3 medium	4 cups chopped
Potatoes, white, red, russet	1 pound	4 cups chopped
Rice	1 cup regular	3 cups cooked
	1 cup instant	2 cups cooked
	1 cup brown	4 cups cooked
	1 cup wild	4 cups cooked
Shortening	1 pound	2½ cups
Shrimp	1 pound shelled	2 cups cooked
	1 pound in shell	20–30 large
		11–15 jumbo
Sour cream	1 cup	1 cup plain yogurt; ¾ cup buttermilk; 1 tbsp. lemon juice plus enough evaporated milk to equal 1 cup
Squash	1 pound summer	3 cups sliced
	1 pound winter	1 cup cooked, mashed
Strawberries	1 pint fresh	1½ cups sliced
	10 ounces frozen	1½ cups
Sugar	1 cup light brown	½ cup packed brown sugar plus ½ cup granulated sugar
	1 cup granulated	1¾ cups confections sugar; 1 cup packed brown sugar; 1 cup superfine sugar
	1 pound granulated	2 cups
	1 pound confectioners	3½ cups
	1 pound brown	2¼ cups packed
Tomatoes	3 medium	1½ cups chopped
Tomato juice	1 cup	½ cup tomato paste plus ½ cup water
Tomato sauce	1 cup	½ cup tomato paste plus ½ cup water
Vanilla wafers	22 cookies	1 cup crumbs
Wine	750 ml	3 cups
Yogurt	1 cup	1 cup buttermilk; 1 cup plus 1 tbsp. lemon juice

Index

Recipe Names & Categories

D

● ●

To Order: *365 Fast Easy Recipes*

Please send _____ hardcover copies @ $19.95 (U.S.) each $ _____

Texas residents add sales tax @ $1.60 each $ _____

Please send _____paperback copies @ $16.95 (U.S.) each $ _____

Texas residents add sales tax @ $1.34 each $ _____

Plus postage/handling @ $6.00 (1st copy) $ _____

$1.00 (each additional copy) $ _____

Check or Credit Card (Canada-credit card only) **Total** $ _____

Charge to: **Mail or Call:**

_____ MasterCard _____Visa   Cookbook Resources

Account # _____   541 Doubletree Drive

Expiration Date _____   Highland Village, Texas 75077

Signature_____   Toll Free (866) 229-2665

Fax (972) 317-6404

Name _____

Address_____

City_____State_____Zip _____

Telephone (Day)_____(Evening)_____

• •

To Order: *365 Fast Easy Recipes*

Please send _____ hardcover copies @ $19.95 (U.S.) each $ _____

Texas residents add sales tax @ $1.60 each $ _____

Please send _____paperback copies @ $16.95 (U.S.) each $ _____

Texas residents add sales tax @ $1.34 each $ _____

Plus postage/handling @ $6.00 (1st copy) $ _____

$1.00 (each additional copy) $ _____

Check or Credit Card (Canada-credit card only) **Total** $ _____

Charge to: **Mail or Call:**

_____ MasterCard _____Visa   Cookbook Resources

Account # _____   541 Doubletree Drive

Expiration Date _____   Highland Village, Texas 75077

Signature_____   Toll Free (866) 229-2665

Fax (972) 317-6404

Name _____

Address_____

City_____State_____Zip _____

Telephone (Day)_____(Evening)_____